Mitak's incomplete

Be somebody,

I needed love and care,
But something told me I needed somebody there,
I need to be somebody on top,
Need to shine until my heart stops,

Listen to what I'm about to say,
Listen carefully to the words that I'll portrait,
I can talk about money, cars, girls or
Whatever people say these days,

But I rather talk about real pain,
Rather talk about real stuff,
Rather talk about real tears,

Sometimes I hate myself,
Sometimes I love myself,
I breathe in all the pain hoping
That I'll harm myself,
And then eventually kill myself,

Man I've been here couple times,

And I've heard all the fake promises and lies,
Just to get one message across,
I have to put these words in a rhyme,

It's like no matter what I say,
These people don't understand,
You don't see the struggle around you,
Only care about yourself,
That's the thing I can't stand,

In this pale world I have to be the colour,
The world is my canvas,
I'm the paint brush,
That's going to fill it with colour,

I'm going to paint, paint and paint until the world changes,
Because I'm going to change the world,
No more pain, no more living in cages,
That's me, that's what I'm saying,

These are emotions that are put into words,
Written on the page,
And made it into a verse,
Feel like my whole life is backwards,
There are no second chances,
This is it; this is where I start,

The only respect you get is when there are roses on your grave,
It feels like I died,
I'm just getting by day by day,
So tell me why they say no racism,
But we're still separated by race,

This is where you'll hear my story,
This is where you'll know about my life,
This is where you'll know about my pain, my tears, and my cries.

-Written at age 14.

"People don't realise how a man's whole life can be changed by one book." – Malcom X

My mum always used to say that the reason why she was going through all these bad things in her life,
"It is because something amazing is coming for me. Something really good is going to happen to me, I know it!".

It was those lines that saved me. They got me where I am today. If it wasn't for her inspirational and wise words I would have given up a long time ago. I would have committed suicide. Now I am thankful I didn't.

We listen to people that do not benefit us or share valuable knowledge but when a person speaks with inspiration and wisdom, we blatantly and maybe unknowingly, choose to ignore. Why?. Maybe because ignorance is really a bliss.
It feels like I am dying slowly and no matter what, I can't help but destroy everything around me. It feels like the longer I stand in the light the more my darkness surrounds me.

This book will show you a side that not many people get to know about me, hardly anyone gets to see this side to me. So don't be surprised with what you're about to read. Do not think that this is what makes me weak because, trust me, this is my greatest strength. It has made me who I am today. They told me no one will be interested in my story; they told me I won't be able to do it. But guess what? I went ahead and did it anyway. I wrote a whole book because I kept fighting and because I have a strong belief that my story will motivate people and change lives.

This is my story. My rise to the top. This is my journey to success.

'If you want something in this life go and grab it!'

Invisible sky

Invisible sky, invisible sky,
sometimes you crumble, sometimes you cry.

Why are you always mixed with emotions can't you
choose one part,
Confusion is fine but finding the answer is art,

Invisible sky, invisible sky,
sometimes you crumble, sometimes you cry.

Don't tell me the truth if your only going to lie, and don't
curse at me when your only going to smile,

Invisible sky, invisible sky,
sometimes you crumble, sometimes you cry.

"I say self made, meaning I design myself." - Nipsey
Hussle

I don't know how long I'll be alive. I think my time is near
and it will be time for me to go home soon. You know that
feeling, as if god put those feelings to let you know it's
time. Like he is telling you to hurry up, finish and go home
to him. I don't know if I'll be gone before this book gets
published or after. But I just want everyone to pray for
me. Pray that I make it out this dark place I'm suffocating
in. If I'm already gone - please, pray for my well-being no
matter where I am.

I'm hoping this book impacts people's lives - which is the
main reason why I wrote it and shared my life experience.

I took my time writing this book. I wanted it to be really powerful, meaningful and life changing. I probably won't be alive to see this book go worldwide, maybe I will, who knows. I always felt like I was running out of time, which is why those that know me might have noticed why I'm always in a rush to get things done. I'm not asking for money and I'm not asking for fame, I am just patiently waiting for my time to come so I can leave this world. I am no longer attached to this world by worldly desires. I don't care about that, none of those things matter to me. All that matters is going back home.

'My mind is drowning in a realm where the valley of shadows is called home'.

This is my incomplete and this will remain incomplete till the day I die and when that happens then this story will become complete. I hope to leave an insight through my writing, so read on to see what happens...

When I say I've been through a lot I'm not just talking

about the circumstances and situations I went through, but everything from mentally and emotionally. The battle I'm still fighting inside me, which is what I'm talking about.

'Don't let people know too much about you'.

It's okay if people know about me, because what you will read is the old me. What you will read will paint a picture of how I developed into the new unstoppable me. You will read the journey of how I became the man I am today. All this was therapy for me, more like training, felt like I did time in prison training to fight an even bigger fight. Grind plus time, persistence and consistence is the only way to shine.

Who would have thought that the one who got told he couldn't achieve anything is the one people will be reading about. Who would have thought that the one who didn't have anyone, not even for some guidance would be the one who is guiding people through his writing and words? Who would have thought that the one who was labelled as a failure and almost gave up is the one telling you to be unstoppable? Everything is possible if you set your mind to it.

Just let me die,

There were times I contemplated suicide,

Tried biting my tongue tried holding my breath,

But every time I tried,

All I could see is my mums smile,

I couldn't do it

Couldn't end it,

Life didn't let me do it,

Life wanted success for me,

But I couldn't see it,

Negativity & motivation all wired,

Thought my time came but I was renewed, way before I was expired,

Round after round fight after fight, I've been training so let's go,

I will not fear any longer,

Let life destroy me and I'll come back stronger,

I'm tired of everyone selling me dreams,

Tired of hearing all the struggle screams,

I know all this helped me make a change,

But honestly I just need something to sooth my pain,

Pouring out All this anger and rage,

It helped write all this down on a page,

Fighting battles,

It was this war that I waged,

I became better I've changed,

Stuck in this fantasy stuck in this cage,

I'm trying to help everyone

Success made,

But it seems like I'm the one who I can't save,

There was a time I was living in a room with nothing but a bed and a fridge. I was struggling with money. Most of the time I went to sleep starving because I didn't have enough money to buy some food. The hunger became a pain I couldn't bear. It was so bad that the pain spread to my chest. I always thought that this will be the last pain I'll feel.

Values:

'People will always have something to say whether it's positive or negative, but that's not the bad thing. The bad thing is when you start to listen and actually pay attention, that's when you lose.'

People are always going to have something to say no matter what you do. So might as well do what you want to do. That shouldn't stop you from doing the things you love. Stop caring about what others think and start caring about what you think and feel.

I stand up for those that have been through pain, those that have been through a lot, those that are too afraid to speak up I stand for them. I stand for their better future, I stand for their pain to be heard, for their cries to be heard, I stand up for those that want freedom suffering. You might take my life, you might take my freedom but you can't take my soul.

Goals:

If you are already working on your goals and pouring your heart out into what you love doing - you are winning. If you haven't already started then you are falling behind. Stop waiting for things to happen and make them happen now! Nothing will magically fall from the sky. Whether you are in a relationship, whether you are in love, nothing will progress until you decide to go do something about it. Stop fearing what will happen, focus on the moment you are in now and worry about the future later. Don't let failures hold you back. Don't let rejections put you down. You don't need the flashy lights and cameras to tell you that you are successful. You don't need 7 or more digits in your bank account to tell you that you are successful. Trust me you don't need that! So work on your goals and stay winning!

Day one, one day, what's the difference

I'm going to be big one day,

And I know it,

This is my destiny,

That's how I saw it,

Give happiness to my pain,

Because I owe it,

Never will I fail,

Because I already been through it,

And if I die right now,

I'll be happy because I lived,

Like one of the greatest and the realest,

To ever live.

'People say one day I want to have this, I want to be in this place or this is who I want to be. The way I see it is, the day you start doing everything you can and start working towards your one day, that is when your day one of the journey to one day starts.'

It all began with...

My life began with a peaceful and a happy start. Those days when you're just a little innocent baby that has no idea of what the future holds. Those days were the best days where there is no pain, no stress, and no worries; just laying down sleeping on your bed in your mother's arms peacefully. Those were the days. Looking back at them now I wish I was a kid again, on second thoughts forget that, I just remembered that during my childhood I wasn't the happiest child. In fact I wasn't happy at all. Few months before I was born my dad sent a letter to my mum's dad. On the letter he wrote the way he will treat my mum. Just like ripped up sandals, he will keep mum under his feet. In other words, he will keep mum like a slave and treat her like dirt.

It's messed up I know.

He also wrote on that letter that he'll make sure there are always tears in her eyes and her nose is always watery from crying all the time.

At this point my mother became a woman with no right to live and a woman with no power. My mother went to her new husbands home with dreams and hopes of starting a new life. Who would have thought life had other plans for her. My granddad was shocked, disgusted and angry that he just gave his daughter to an evil, vile being that has no heart. My granddad was going through a lot of emotions all at once. He was hurt and worried for his daughter.

One day, granddad said to mum, "this is your life and this is your choice so you decide what you want to do. But remember this, as long as this man is in your life you'll never have a happy home and you will never be happy". Mum still contemplates her father's words until this day.

Granddad left my mum with an option to realise that this man is not the one for her. But through it all, when my mum became pregnant with me in her tummy, everyone was looking forward to meeting me. On the day I was born my granddad woke up early in the morning, just after sunrise, got on the bus and made his way to the hospital. At his old age it was really hard to travel, especially in Bangladesh. Back then travel facilities were not great. But he was too excited to see his grandchild. He came to the hospital and immediately began searching for me and even held me once he found me. When I think about this, I come to a realisation. That even though my granddad was filled with happiness, he felt hurt because he knew the future I was coming into. He was worried for the days that I'll be growing up.

Today, he is no longer here but I know that my granddad was absolutely right.

Then the day came, when I was 5. I saw my dad hit my mum countless times. I couldn't resist any longer, I went and told my granddad. That's when he said enough is enough and I came to the UK without my parents. To this day, I have not seen them since.

"Sometimes I really hate myself, sometimes I wish that I could change myself, sometimes I don't want to give no more and sometimes I just don't want to live no more.

Sometimes I just don't know where to go for help, sometimes I don't really know myself, sometimes I wish that I could fly away and find a way to a brighter day." - Lowkey

'You will never be successful if you are afraid to be alone.'

Growing up:

To me and I think to everyone family is the most important thing in this world. Growing up for me was really hard. I was missing that mother and father love from my childhood. People underestimate me and always look down on me, I was never understood by anyone and never got that help and guidance that I really needed. If I did get any it would be about how to get good grades and that you should focus on your school work. But how was I supposed to focus on my work when all this pain and tiring thoughts kept running circles in my brain. How was a little kid suppose to cope with all that pain and suffering.

Gold, Diamonds, Syrup & Almonds

Drown in gold or swim in diamonds,
Sweet syrup and soft almonds,

I Live, I Sell or I trade in,
I Taste the vision,
Before I need saving,

I'm going to be successful
& it's true,
Wrote it down
And it's all becoming true,

Sometimes I wonder where my life will go,
Sometimes I wonder if I should let them know,
Or keep quiet
And let this progression grow,

There was a time
I couldn't find God,
Like every time I called
No one answered my line,

Couldn't understand his plan,
Why am I going through this
And why he stop me,
Because what I'm about to do

I'll loose everything,

I'm like that painting on the wall
Just for show, watch me,
Because you will never know
How many colours it took to
Make me,

I'm living like the last few,
I Hustle without any plug,
What's a plug
when your fuse all blown up,

What's a plug
When the powers all gone,
And what's hustle
When you feel like you got no chance,

Maybe it's this brown skin
That tells them I'm nothing more then dirt,
Hungry, sick and mentally rich,
Cream and cookies
A sweet appetising sin,

Maybe we should stop talking about
Who's the next big hit,
And talk about what's the next
Big problem that's going to hit,

Forget that we haven't even fixed our
Last problems,
Like world hunger and poverty,
Its probably because your too busy
Complaining about a rich man
not paying enough taxes,

Can't blame you
That's what happens when
School doesn't teach you about money,
Living pay check to pay check,
Maybe your just a slave with a salary,

I'm a visionary, in my visions,
I'm a mercenary, with my own mercy,
With my success I will reign,
A new man every time after
Every storm and rain,

Drown in gold or swim in diamonds,
Sweet syrup and soft almonds,

I Live, I Sell or I trade in,
I Taste the vision,
Before I need saving,

I've always felt like a failure. As if no matter what I do, nothing will go the way I planned it to go. Eventually everyone ends up leaving me behind. They don't give a second look to see if I'm okay. However, the more I tell my story to people the more people start to understand me and now I see that I should have done this years ago. Maybe my life wouldn't have been so difficult to deal with if I did. Then maybe I wouldn't have been forced to carry all the weight of the world on my shoulders.

I have the craziest motivational energy. A hunger for success. I believe this is because I know the struggle I had to go through. If it was up to me, I would want to live a simple life with just the right amount food on the plate, a little family with me and my wife. Not worrying about living luxuriously. You know that saying - more money, more problems?. That's why.
Unfortunately I can't have that life because of all the

people that underestimated me. Especially the people in my inner circle like my family. It's a tough burden to carry when your close ones have no belief, faith or trust in you. I lacked that support. This is where my motivation comes from - I want to prove everyone wrong and show them that I can become someone. Someone successful.

"Somebody told me I'm a failure! I'll prove them wrong!" - Uzumaki Naruto.

When I was at my lowest, with no money, or no sense of home, I could never picture that I will become the person I am today.

Don't ever let anyone define who you are, you are in charge of your life. Don't listen to what anyone says whether it's good or bad don't listen because what they have to say it does not matter it will only put you down and slow you down. You just have to make sure you, yourself, already know that you are successful and don't let anyone tell you otherwise!!

I love the life I live because I went from negative to positive and it's all good.

Every memory you have, every thought you have comes with a cost, a cost of feeling pain.

When people feel pain, see pain, hear pain, taste pain and know pain that's when people will realise the true meaning of how it feels to be happy. It's like saying in order to know the meaning of happiness you must first know the meaning of pain.

Sometimes I feel like breaking down and just sit there alone and cry, sometimes I don't feel like talking I get sick of talking about the same things over and over again. I feel like if I could just rip open my body and show everyone what is inside then only they would understand.

But you know all these things that have happened to me and what I had to go through has made me much stronger and wiser. I now know that in order to get some respect and appreciation I need to make something of myself I need to prove to the world that they have made a mistake for underestimating me and I will make the world know the true meaning of pain and the true meaning of happiness.

I'm on a mission to change the world to make this a better place and most importantly a mission to make my mother happy and proud of me, to make this a place where you don't be judged easily, where people look at you equally, where you can stand on your two feet without having someone knock you over by intelligence, by beauty or by status. Everyone has their own story to tell but I will make sure everyone knows my story and everyone knows what I have done to change the world. People will know me as the man who changed the world.

This isn't the saddest story I ever told. This is just life and I must live this. Everything is relative we all live the same drama just different levels of hardships. Is this just a dream? Am I just fool for trying? Well if that is the case then I'll be the biggest fool that the world will know of, because I'm not going to give up. Will my visions be reality they tell me never? I will rise!! I said I will rise!! We will rise!!

When I talk about changing the world I don't mean it literally, what I mean is that there will be people out there living better because they will know the way they can change themselves; most importantly they will know how to reach that level of success.

"No matter what you do, your job is to tell your story."-
Gary Vaynerchuk

Colourless

Are you colourful or
are You colourless,

I got brown skin & I got black hair,
And I got a beard
so I'm a target,

They call you black,
They call me a terrorist,
so racism still exists,
is this something we can't resist,

I thought we was the same damn,
Its funny because there is more shades to us
then a white man,

So what makes them more superior to us,

Am I racist? Maybe I am,
But aren't we all
if colour is the only way
to define who I Am?

I see how they look at me
when I'm speaking from my lungs,
And how they get scared
when I'm speaking my mother tongue,

So what's the difference,

Black or religion,
Hatred or loving,
Life or living,
Slavery or freedom,

Killing and winning,
Sinning and grinning,

Are you colourful or
Are you colourless,

Knife crime,
terror crime,

Black on black
Murder crime,

When will this stop
when will it be more then fine,
When will it be that time
when we stop saying never mind,

When will it be that time when we say,
Whether you are colourful or colourless,
We all breathe the same air
And we all have live this thing called life.

Are you colourful or
Are you colourless.

'The worst form of isolation you can be in, is in your own
mind.'

Primary Life

Through my primary life I have always focused on my studies even though it was hard for me with all that was going on at home but I still managed to get through it and came out with really good grades on my SAT.

I remember around year 4 and year 5 we had really good classmates. Everyone was so nice and funny. We all got a long really well. Everyone was friends our whole class, the atmosphere in our classes was amazing. Our teachers were nice and understandable. Every lunch time we used to play football and I remember once I hurt my arm really badly completely grazing my skin off. I still have the mark today near my left elbow. At first it hurt so badly and then I felt cool like I just had a battle with a death eater from Harry Potter. In a way I was glad, looking back at it now, because I have something to remind me of a memory I had in my childhood.

We played other fun games that all my friends made up. I loved going to primary it was the best place to be if I had a choice to go back now I would definitely go. No stress, no worries, no responsibilities. Just have the freedom to be a child and enjoy the colourful dimensions full of adventures.

By the time I was in year six I became one of the popular ones, in fact I think everyone in my year was popular we all knew each other including other years knowing who we were. In year six it was a bit stressful at the start of the year because we had our Sat exams coming up and we had to decide what secondary school we wanted to attend. We had revisions classes every day after school and some of them were fun like the science one. We had to play with toy cars on different types of materials to learn about friction.
Dropping a book with a paper to see which one lands first, testing Newton's discovery of gravity.

Maths was really boring although our teacher kept having fisherman cough sweets for his throat and nose. He gave us some time to time it was really strong but I kind of liked it. We learnt about all the interesting facts and stories about dinosaurs and cavemen. We learnt about the different types of animals and how the world came to be through nature. I loved it. It gave my entrepreneurial young mind even more ideas to how the world could be like in the future.

'Never forget the sacrifices that got you where you are today.'

Although I always told myself I was going to be successful one day I didn't really give it much thought at the time as I was busy just enjoying the happy childhood I was missing, even if it's just a little moment of happiness. It will take me away from the darkness my mind was drowning in. These happy moments make me forget about everything else and also show that there are positives to your life no matter how negative it may seem.

Growing up without my parents around took away all my possibilities of being happy. However if at that age I knew it was down to me to change that no one else. But somehow I still chose to loose myself rather than escape from this misfortune. Even when my social workers used to visit me I would tell them I'm okay, everything is going good. You know the usual I'm fine act. If I told them I'm not okay they would have took me and put me in care, because they would see I'm not happy there. Who would have thought that 7 years down the line I did end up going into care, because things did not work out with the family I was meant to live with. You can sit and list all the bad things that are happening right now or you can look for the positives and make the most of it. Any time you are feeling in the dark, stop and think about all the times in your life you was happy. Think back to all your happy memories that you have had. Yes this might make you feel like you want to go back, but now what you need to do is think about how you can make more of those memories again. Make more of those happy memories with what you have now.

The reason why I wrote this memory is to show that there is a good side to everything; it only comes down to you how you view it as. It is your choice to make it into a negative situation or you can turn that around and make it positive.

For once let's stop naming all the problems that we have in our life and start naming all the blessings that we have. Like a family, a mum, a dad, people that love us, food, shelter, water, clothes, our hands, our feet, our eyes to see, our ears to hear, our mouth to speak and eat.

Every day you have to wake up feeling content, appreciative, humble and thankful for being alive and healthy. Every day is a new day. This is your Chance to move on. Forget about what happened yesterday. Start new.

We have to learn how to take care of others it's not just about ourselves. If we all took care of one another imagine how different society itself would be. In today's world there is no greetings, no conversations about what we love, what we want to do, just learning about one and another. We are too distracted from Worldly desires. Why don't we try and speak to the person next to us on the train instead of staring at our phones being awkward. "Hi, how are doing." "How was your day?" "So, where are you going today, any plans?" Sentences like this saves lives trust me. It creates new relationships, open doors of opportunities for you and also gives you the chance to communicate with people, improving all your personal skills including confidence.

It shows that you care for others well enough to go out your way to know how someone else is doing. Try it, I'll tell you right now watch how good you feel after that talk. I remember my first day in secondary school it was different for me the environment and the atmosphere. It was hard for me because I didn't know anyone there and I felt scared, it felt like I was some new born baby that just came into the world.

After my parents left me my heart was hurting and I was missing them so much I felt like crying all the time, everyone felt like strangers to me all I wanted was my mum. I was a child that needed his mum. I would see other kids with their mum and dad, picking them up from school and dropping them to school. I always had that feeling like I was missing someone from my life I was missing my mum and dad.

When I think back to this it brings tears to my eyes and every time I think of this I feel like crying, even while I'm writing this now I'm dropping so many tears. The pain that built up from my childhood still remains with me till this day, the fact that I couldn't have my mum and dad through my childhood hurts me so much, the fact that I couldn't come home and say mum I'm home. Ever since I was little I knew my destiny was great that I was here for a reason that all the things that had happened to me was for a reason I knew that I will be someone big in the future no matter what path I take it will lead me to that greatness and success.

'When we have nothing, we have nothing to loose. So why are we still afraid?'

I never had anything, I probably will never get any recognition or even recognised for what I'm about to do. I probably will never get that appreciation or an award for the things I will do. All I wanted was a decent life you can't even imagine what I had to go through. When life gets real and your stuck there is nothing you can really do. I probably won't get known or celebrated for being the person I am. I'm only saying that because the world we live in today, people ignore these sorts of things. No one wants to talk about the fight through the darkness. People rather pay attention to those that do silly things on social media. You'll see that all these people will become famous and get their praise. And here is real people like me trying to do something better for the world and we don't get nothing. They don't even know we exist.

Stop listening to pointless mumble rap and stop listening to these idiots that talk nonsense, stop copying these people because you think they look cool. Stop rewarding these pointless individuals that do stupid acts or make a silly looking dance. There are real problems out there in the world. Wake up!

Start rewarding people that are doing all they can to make this world a better place to live. Reward those that are helping people no questions asked. They are the real ones who you should be watching at 2 am in the night.

People like that should get all the awards for their amazing work.
I know maybe I will never be one of those but that will not stop. So long as God gives me breath for years to come I will pour my heart out in to becoming successful, showing

others how to do it and helping anyone I can.

'From a child I was told I could never be someone great and big, my reply was silence because my actions will speak for me.'

Get comfortable with rejections because that's one powerful tool. When your heart breaks you mind will work like it's never worked before. That's the best time to take all of the bad emotions and negative thoughts, turn it into something positive. Use that new energy that you have just created and create something amazing. It's so disappointing to see people my age taking advantage of everything they have. If only they can see, how lucky they are to have all of those things. Like a family, a stable future because you have your family behind you and don't have that much worries and responsibilities because your dad or mum handles all the bills. These are just few examples but you know what I mean.

Young people nowadays just go to college or university, work a part time job and that's it. They go out most of the times and just have fun. Don't get me wrong I'm not against having fun. If you can see from my perspective with all the things I had to go through. For all the sacrifices and hard work I had to put in to get to where I am just because I was in a much more disadvantage than everyone else.

So what I'm trying to say is that people like that young people that have a lot of advantage and that are lucky to have that, should be doing more and it should be way more easier. Because they have support and because they have everything that I ever wanted but I was not so lucky.

You don't just want to do college or university, get a degree, get a full time job, work for 40 years, and then retire after paying off all your debts. Now that's a future I would not want for myself. When you are young it's the best time to get yourself out there and be doing the things you love. Yes go to university, get your qualifications I'm not saying don't do that. However what I'm saying is that you should be working on something amazing at the same time. Do something you love, something that makes you happy, something you want to be doing the rest of your life and make a living from it.

Don't make it too late and don't wait till you get put into a place where you no longer see anything else but regrets. Because even though you are lucky and have everything soon or later that luck runs out, when you don't appreciate and give it the love it deserves.

Sometimes I feel like I need to do something else. I get bored with the life I live the same routine over and over again. And what makes it worse? Is that I'm doing something which I completely dislike. Most people give up a few steps away from achieving their goals.

"The future belongs to those who prepare for it today". – Malcom X

King of miseries

God, give me strength,

Give me courage & let me atone,

I am the king of miseries,

So give me my throne,

Shall I rain down havoc

Or should it be a mixture,

With your permission,

Let me lead my people out of this hell-hole,

Let me be that vessel that carries the darkness,

Let me be that warrior that eradicates all negativity,

I will give orders

And I'll follow my heart,

I will make promises

And I won't lie,

I will find peace

And I won't tear it apart,

I'll sit on my throne,

So hand me down my rights,

I have made my army,

And they are ready for any strife,

God, give me strength,

Give me courage & let me atone,

I am the king of miseries,

So give me my throne.

What's my reason?

For me happiness is when my mother smiles, so that is why I have to be someone big in the future and make my mum proud so wherever she is in the world she could smile and be proud of me. Once I fly I won't be coming back I'm going to fly towards that blue sky and there's no stopping me.

As the years passed by I don't know what happened to me and how all of a sudden my grades went down I begun to focus less in class. I didn't know if it was because of friends or if I just didn't really have any interest left with school.

The fact that I didn't have my mum and dad there with me throughout my childhood it affected me in many ways even till this day If my aunty or anyone that know me closely would be like what you talking about you were fine during those times but what people don't realise that hardships and pain can make someone put a mask on and pretend it's all happy days. Those days was not going well for me, I always used to hide my feelings and never show how I'm really feeling. I'm that type of person that loves getting attention and I hate when I be ignored or that feeling when you're not there.

I always felt like people don't really like me I'm just like a germ or a disease that no one wants to catch. I think that impression came to me when I was labelled as the abandoned lonely no good for nothing dumb clown boy.

Usually as the years progressed and I became more and

more depressed and upset I started having thoughts that I shouldn't have been having. In my life I've met so many people, people that have helped like Arrival Education and others that just threw dirt on my face. I'm quiet and I don't say much you could say I am man of few words, I think pain and the heartbreaks have made me this way I keep everything in my head and I like to stay to myself.

Being successful was something I always had in mind. It was a goal that has not left me and is still with me today. Many people have different definitions of what success is to them. For me, it's being able to say I'm happy with where I am right now. It is not so hard to achieve success as long as you don't let your fears overpower you and defeat you. Most people vision success to be something you will see in a film, where the main character will become an overnight success after getting some sort of power. I'm sorry to tell you that, this does not happen in real life. Instead what people should be like is the rebel in star wars where they fight for what they want to make sure they are happy. I don't want to do this for myself but I want to leave a legacy behind so the next generation and the next generation can have a better life, I want to do this so my children, children, children can live in a less havoc world.

I'm at that point in my life where I am still trying to learn how to forgive, I'm still trying to forgive my parents for leaving me but now I can say that in a way I'm happy that they did because I wouldn't be the person I am today. The experiences and the pain I felt has made me much stronger and understand more about everything and how everything works.

When people don't believe in you and have faith in you, let me tell you that is a lonely feeling. If it was easy to achieve success then everyone would have been doing it, most people are satisfied with the life they have, and most people are going to work doing a job that they don't like why? Because they are scared of trying, scared of failing. Most people die and take their dreams with them to the grave. That's why I say the graveyard is the richest place in the world because there are inventions, ideas, dreams and goals that never happened. Those dreams have died with some great minds, that never got the chance to discover what they were hiding inside. Just because they were scared to chase their dreams and just gave in to the easy life they were already living. Don't be that person, don't be afraid to take a step which you've never taken before, don't be afraid to step out your comfort zone and most importantly don't be afraid to fail!! DON'T BE AFRAID TO FALL!! Because when you fall you'll have to land somewhere, you can't fall forever. Trust me the fall is worth it even if it is a little difference it becomes a big part of your life later on you might not realise it now, but one day you'll look back and just smile.

Honey Hive

Oh demon men, oh demon men,
Protect your clan from the sacred lie,
For the devils men
Loves her honey hive,

Yes I got some skeletons in the closet,
And I got some monsters under my bed,
While Demons watch me sleep,
Angels want me dead,

While my spirit flies,

My body decays for a mili second,
My brain lags like a broken computer chip,
It's that place where my dreams get beheaded,

What is this sorrow,
What is this sadness,
What is tomorrow,
When your airless & hollow,

Look at my crimes,
Look at my injustice,
Look at my culture,
Look at my rights,

I'm confused, why do I bleed on the rug
But in front of the mirror I don't cry,
Why does their blood soak up,
while my becomes vile,

In this life I've never owned anything of mine,
but yet the devils man loves her honey hive,
yet they want to give me everything,
but I decline for it will poison and destroy life,

Oh demon men, oh demon men,
Protect your clan from the sacred lie,

For the devils men
Loves her honey hive,

Angels are crying,
Devils are smiling,
It's their world,
Behind the scenes their the ones wining,

Everyday I dig my grave and take a nap in it,
just so I get a taste of what death is,
I thought life was meaningless,
Until I saw my breath illuminate,

I shiver spontaneously,
While this fragrance is actually horrendous,
I search for equations,
As I'm trapped in this fuliginous,

I feel invisible,
But at the same time lamentable,
desiring a new home,
Before I feel regrettable,

What is this differentiation,
What is this calamity,
What is this cruelty,

What is this insanity,

Am I just a fragment of energy,
following this hypocrisy,
Without a purpose,
We have no necessity,

So tell the demon men,
And tell the devils tale of the Honey hive,
For I don't answer to no one,
Expect to my creator who is always by my side.

Oh demon men, oh demon men,
Protect your clan from the sacred lie,
For the devils men
Loves her honey hive.

The Purpose is to be happy!

The purpose is to be happy. Whatever it is you are doing? Whoever you are trying to be? Remember this; the purpose is to be happy! That means if something does not make you feel good, does not make you happy let that go, you don't want that any more. No matter what, in fact you know there and then, no! That's not for me full stop. That's it! Yes I'm also talking about the people not just the materialistic things in this world but the people as well.

If this certain type of person does not make you happy or being around this person does not make you happy or this person does not make you happy at all? Then stop and get yourself out of there because the purpose is to be happy. Say it! My purpose is to be happy. This also means I just don't need to be happy but feel happy; mentally and physically I need to be healthy and have a clear positive happy mind. Stop being that miserable person that wishes every day for a miracle to happen where you will magically feel happy because that will never happen no one just feels happy out of nowhere. You have to create that yourself find what makes you happy and do what makes you happy. You need to have a positive energy, a clear mind and healthy routine. Being happy takes time, sometimes it does not, depending on you, how badly do you want it? A small step means big step doing little things that makes you feel good and makes you happy.

Doing something nice for someone else, helping someone you care about, and being there for someone, working hard with a smile, having a clear heart free from jealousy and anger. A good intention for the life you want to live. Having patience and being humble, appreciating the blessings you already have. Always remember something wonderful is about to happen. Be who you want to be, do what you want to do, be happy within, because happiness is your purpose for living. Remember, the purpose is to be happy

Where I'm at with my life right now- 2015

Right now in my life I'm at Arrival working, I dropped out of my second year of college as I had to face difficulties trying to enrol and I really didn't want to stay in college any more as I didn't see no interest in it any more. There was a lot happening for me at that time. From the beginning it was written I suppose, they not going to love me for whom I am but for who I'm destined to be!!

Do you ever get that feeling where you don't know what you're doing any more like your mind just goes blank? Sometimes in life you just have to deal with certain things and sometimes you just have to step out of the fantasy, come back to reality and accept whatever you are going through.

I've started writing this book and hopefully would like to publish it one day. At this point of my life I don't really know what it is exactly I want to do. Maybe it is too early to tell.

You know deep down inside I do care about what people think about me, like I mean when they say bad things about me. I start believing it and start ignoring myself and start listening to their opinions. However I know this is something that I have to fight and improve myself on so that in the future it won't matter to me any more what anyone thinks of me. But to get to that level I know I would have to keep developing myself and increase my positive energy.

Just like what you read at the start of this book, that this story of mine will not only motivate you but also show you the journey of how I become better over the years. It will show you the growth and battles I had to go through and how I change.

Does freedom exist?

We talk about freedom

But yet we are afraid to be free,

We live in chains

In a jungle that's disguised by concrete,

We say we love ourselves

But yet we lack self-esteem,

And we say we do the things we love

But yet instead we are what the world told us to be,

So tell us what you want

Is it love or sympathy?

You should walk through the valley of death

Look death in the face,

Tell them what you have been through

And tell them what you have witnessed,

My skin rips open crying blood tears

Losing too much blood is what it fears,

Maroon & black cells dancing away

Shaken up by a loud pulse it hears,

That's my heart beating

Wow that was close,

Thought I died

Thought my heart just froze,

I can't believe it!

That's my tear from a while ago,

I dropped it when I was 7

But why is it here for?

It's bringing back all these memories

Stop! It's hurting me I can't help it,

A needle going through my brain

Yes that was my migraine,

Why can't I escape?

Why can't I be free?

I'm in control

But yet I fear originality,

I limit myself

But my mind is something without an end,

Why are these emotions laughing?

Saying this is how it begins,

What do they mean?

Are they talking about humans destroying something?

Is it how humans are destroying humanity?

And turning reality upside down saying it's within?

It's a cinematic reality

Crushed with a smile just grinning,

They think this is how it's meant to be

That this is called living,

But little do they know

That they are not trying to die,

That's all humans are doing

For every step they take everything multiplies,

Now all the negativity has entered your life

How can you run from yourself? You say suicide,

Your shadows surround you

And copy you,

They say we are so happy your about to die

We always hated you,

This is us being true,

We're finally going to be free

For the entire trauma you put us through,

Now was there a choice between

Depression or happiness

I could have made a choice

I didn't need to live according to the pyramid,

Every night I wonder today my life could change,

Laying in the dark all I could see

Is the light in the maze?

You say you want to be free

And live a life like your dream,

But yet you don't listen to your soul

You rather listen to your screams.

Emmanuel Stevens- The best Mentor & Friend

Wow I don't know where to start about you Emmanuel. I know that you are excited to read this book more than anyone I know. I mean you were the one who told me to carry on and write this book just when I was about to give up. Let me just start by saying thank you for everything you have done for me, Emmanuel. You have been the best mentor and friend to me. The guidance and advice I received from you over the years have helped me so much. Believe It or not when I was in a dark space you were the only person I could go to and I know I won't be judged or be viewed as a "freak".

I felt like you understood me and knew exactly what to say to me at the right moment. Whenever I came to you with problems you always showed me solutions and what I liked best is that you never let me use your examples, you made me figure out my own solutions. That helped me so much because it taught me how to think effectively and come up with solutions soon as a problem occurs. It also taught me to learn the hard way and find out how I can stand on my own two feet.

Yes it was Emmanuel that got me to start YouTube, that I should do what I love and enjoy and follow my dreams. He was the one that believed in me and always says that one day I will become so successful. I remember one day we spoke for hours, at first we spoke about what was bothering me, why do I want to give up, why am I struggling to make things happen and what is it that I really want? That conversation went from me being negative and having massive anxiety about my life and about the future, to a conversation where we started talking about crazy ideas and innovations that we can create for the future. We came up with so many ideas and we were talking about how we can't wait to work with each other in the future. Maybe have a really successful business that we can run together and set up different cool projects around the world.

It was Emmanuel that told me I need to document everything I do in my life. Even if people are not watching the content I'm putting out there it should be mainly for me to watch. So in the future I can look back at these materials and see how far I've come. It's also proof that I didn't become successful from luck but from hard work, determination, struggle, suffering and being able to come out from the darkness my mind is drowning in. That wasn't all; he also told me that work ethic is the most important thing. If you want something to happen for you then you need to make it happen by putting in work and following it through with action.

 He always used to talk about inventing technologies and he loved doing art. He is so smart and the way he does his work and the way he thinks it's so astonishing. He even showed me how he documented his work on social media such as Instagram. He would display his work so professionally.

I would usually have a meeting every once a month with Emmanuel, to keep updating him on how I am getting on.

If there is anything I need help with he will advise me further. Emmanuel was really motivational as well as determined I remember he used to tell me how he used to go sleep late because he himself is working on his dreams.

He also got me into books. I mean I used to read here and there but he introduced me to what I called self-help books. Just like how you are reading this book right now. He told me about amazing books like "Rich dad, poor dad" and so many other motivational books. And yes you guessed it; I just fell in love with books after that. I started reading Tony Robins "Awaken the giant within", Gary Vaynerchuk "Crushing it" and many more!

Emmanuel helped me way more than he knows himself. All those times I was down and not having well days he always used to advise me in the right way. He was the mentor and friend I needed. Gladly he was there at my darkest times.

I remember when we went to an art gallery in London one day; I thought it was going to the most boring thing in the world. Guess what? I was totally wrong. I loved it! It opened my mind to so many creative things. We even made a lot of content and videos during that day because he wanted me to document my experience and share it. I met Emmanuel when I was about 14 or 15, since then he helped me change my life around and really figure out what I want to do. He showed me that being creative is the best thing you can be. I should do what I want and become successful. He also taught me about money, what is really important in life. In 2015 I begun working for Arrival where Emmanuel was working but I was dong volunteering work. I loved video editing and writing my book. It was in that office that I started writing this book and where I learnt how to edit videos. I started making my vlogs and videos for YouTube. Emmanuel got me to do volunteering work there. I really needed that especially because at that time so many things were going wrong for me, I felt like I wasn't doing anything with my life and anything I tried just kept failing. So working there gave me a sense of reality, made me feel good and made me feel like I am working towards something good.

 In October 2016 at the graduation event, I made my first ever speech at the age of 16 in front of 2,000 people. I went on stage and started speaking about my life straight from the heart. It was the realist moment of my life. I didn't even know I had the guts to speak about something so touching. Emmanuel and Daniel were hosting the whole event. Daniel Snell is the CEO of Arrival Education. I remember my speech was so deep but yet so funny, I kept looking to my side where Emmanuel and Daniel were after I said something funny every time.

I knew this was my first stepping stone to success. For me it was such a big step I took. Emmanuel always taught me to try something new and step out my comfort zone. So I did even though I was nervous it made me want to do so good that people will be talking about me for weeks. I felt like this was my moment so I need to make it count. I wanted people to hear every word and every pain in my voice. I felt like I owed it to my mother and to myself.

Emmanuel made all of this possible for me; it was his guidance, his advice and his connection that was formed from this understanding that made all of this possible. He really gave me that push to overcome my failures and really go after what I want in life.

He always demonstrated the real, he also was going through a lot of problems at that time and he showed me that no matter how wise, how rich or how successful you are, you are always going to have problems and suffering etc. they are never going to go away but what you can do is learn how to deal with it and overcome it. He once told me, think of it this way, I know that within the next week or two something is going to happen. Either I'm going to be stressed, angry, frustrated, struggling or things going wrong. He said as long as you have this in mind you will be fine, because you will be ready so when these do occur you will know exactly how to deal with it.

I was like wow I never thought of it like that. So I tried it and it worked I felt so much better. My fear of failing decreased hugely and I began taking risks and doing what I love regardless.

This is how Emmanuel is thinking and this is how he helped me get onto that mind-set. Now I've built my own mind-set that I follow that works for me and well you can see what it is by reading this book. I give plenty of examples on how I think.

Till this day I am still in touch with Emmanuel and if I had the chance to go back to those days I would certainly go back. We still meet up and talk about what's going on and we both help each other. He has seen me at my worst to how I am now. He has seen how I have developed like literally he has witnessed how I have grown and changed my life around. He has seen first-hand the journey I am going through and the journey that I have gone through so far. And he always says that he is proud of me.

Emmanuel I am so thankful that you were in my life, that you are in my life and that you will carry on being in my life. I don't know how else to thank you for helping me so much. You have helped make a huge difference in my life and I appreciate everything you have done for me. I will always cherish your teachings as well as pass on the knowledge to others.

Me and Emmanuel have a big goal for the future, we want to buy an island and build a city there. Our own society where you don't need to worry about food and survival. It will be just innovations and ideas taking place. Our own education system, our own healthcare systems, our own engineering and architecture plans to build a sustainable place to live. I want to take homeless people, orphans, refugees and anyone else that needs me and give them a place to live. I'll talk more about this futuristic island towards the end of the book.

 I am proud to say that you are one of the best mentors and one of the best friends I have ever had. I can't wait to see what we do in the future and I can't wait to work with you in the future.

Thank you Emmanuel Stevens.

I'm going to be a LEGEND

Like biggie said, it was all a dream,

I used to look at my scars &

Think what my life could be,

I didn't think this could happen,

Success a starter for heaven,

I was a nobody,

wearing the same clothes for weeks,

Eating pot noodles everyday,

Because I didn't have proper food,

Now I'm the king of miseries

Who is living good,

No one to support me through these hard times,

They smile in my face and tell I'm okay,

I used to picture my life loved by millions,

Now I'm closer to my goals,

It's all coming true,

After that day I swore,

I'll never be dependent on anyone,

I'll make my own money & write my own path,

She didn't want to be with me

I was broke and depressed,

Now she wants to be part of my life

And tell me how I'm blessed,

Haha I already knew that,

I'm going to live a legend,

I'm going to die a legend,

They will probably kill me off,

Just like all the greats before me,

I'll probably die with my fist in the sky,

Or a sparkle in my eyes,

I'll go down in history as one of the greatest,

As a legend.

Finding myself

To find yourself and to figure out who you are is the most important thing someone needs to do. If you don't know who you are or don't know anything about yourself then that is the same as saying that you are lost.

If you don't know what kind of person you are, what qualities you have, what strengths and weaknesses you have, what makes you happy, what makes you sad, why do you cry, why do you laugh, why do you smile, why are you kind, why are you rude, then it's fair to say you are nothing but someone that has no meaning, you are someone that is just blank with nothing to write about.

Life is like a box full of chocolates, you just have to find the right ones that taste best to you.

During my childhood I never knew who I was or what kind of a person I really am. I didn't really know myself, I used to feel like I was just some puppet that was dropped on this doorstep, the pain and all the loneliness of being so alone and hurt made me feel like I was meant for all this pain, that this is my life and I must live this, I must bear all the pain and wipe all my tears because no one is here to watch it fall.

I always felt like I was being punished for something I've never done. I felt like this was my punishment and I should just give in.

I was that kind of person that would sacrifice anything just to see someone else happy and I'm still like that. I sacrifice my happiness for pain because in this cold selfish world all I have is pain. When I ever needed a hand, the only hand I had was my hand, every time I fall down because of pain there's only me that lends a helping hand.

It's like that saying when you get kicked down you have to pull yourself back up. Why do we have to rely on ourselves to pick ourselves up? Why don't we have someone there to help us get back to standing up on our own two feet? Why do we only think about ourselves? Why do we only care about ourselves? Why is this world so selfish and so self concerned? That we forget about our fellow brothers and sisters, that we forget what humanity is for.

Knowing yourself doesn't mean you forget and don't care about everyone else?!

I didn't really notice all the amazing qualities that I possess, I only realised it when people started recognising my potentials and telling me what kind of interesting and a special person I really am. I never used to believe them I just used to think that they're only saying that to make me feel better about myself but I soon realised that the only person that can't see this is myself, the only person stopping me from seeing who I really am is myself. The only person that's stopping me is I.

To understand others you must first understand yourself.

Growing up, I was never understood. I was always misunderstood by everyone, no one used to understand the way I feel. No one ever saw the things I had to go through the places my mind visits every day, the kind of tears that fall every night when I'm praying to god with my hands facing the sky.

The only thing people saw was a miserable sad little kid that hates life and everyone in it.

When I talk about my life and my past I feel like I'm complaining and it's just like "oh Mitak get over yourself" but I'm only talking about this so it can help others like me or similar to me. So it shows that other people like me are not alone. I'm here for them. I'm going to help them whether it's through my writing or me physically going out there and offering my hand or wiping their tears away. I want to show the world that who you are is not a bad thing, that you are one extraordinary creation that's waiting to be discovered.

Finding yourself is all about the person you watch yourself become. We don't know how amazing we really are, we as humans can go through so much and still not give up, whatever we go through in life it helps us grow as a person makes us stronger but end of the day it's all entirely up to you.

It's up to you if you want to be happy, it's up to you if you want to change yourself, it's up to you whether you just stop fighting your feelings and let them be, it's up to you to decide to just accept your problems and deal with them instead of trying to run away from them and it's up to you if you want to accept everything including reality and stop pretending that everything is okay or everything is going to be fine when you know deep down that it won't. The only way it will is if you face reality accept it and deal with it until it's solved.

Ask yourself, who am I? What kind of person am I? What kind of person do I want to be? Am I being that kind of person? What is the one thing I really want in life? What is the one thing that will make me happy? Am I happy the way I am? Do I trust others? Do I show my feelings? Do I ask for help? Am I in my fantasy more than I am in my reality? Am I happy the way I am? Am I happy where I am in life right now? Do I need to change? What are these successful people doing differently than me? What have they figured out that I haven't yet? Am I just scared of failure? Do I just give up because it's the easier option? Do I just take short cuts to things? Do I just take the easier way out? Don't I believe in myself and trust myself that I will do well?

Don't I want to be happy and successful?

IF YOU CAN'T FIND HAPPINESS WITHIN YOURSELF HOW DO YOU EXPECT IT TO FIND IT ANYWHERE ELSE?

Life is not about finding you, it's about creating you. So in order to find yourself you must first create yourself. Just remember that it can help you a lot, believe me.

Broken Glass,

I just feel like a broken glass,
So broken don't know if I'll last,
The shattered pieces from my past,
I'm just a broken glass.

Feeling so much pain,
Sometimes I stammer to express myself to the game,
Stressed & broken what do I gain,
Sometimes I love myself,
Sometimes I just think I'm lame,

I'm a deep thinker,
The thoughts in my head are insane,
Can't be living like this any more,
I want to see change,

Tears are words the heart can't say,
So I'll just let the rain,
Wash away the loneliness & pain,

Look into my eyes & you'll see
That I'm not the same,
Guess it's true,
Pain changes you,

I just feel like a broken glass,
So broken don't know if I'll last,
The shattered pieces from my past,
I'm just a broken glass.

I don't feel like talking,
I'm sick of talking,

So much pain & rage in me,
I see the devil everyday every time I look at the mirror
He's there smiling at me,

It's a struggle every day,
Pain, pain, pain is all I ever said,
So much happening in my head,
It's hurting my brain,

Pain is all I got,
Love hurts, turns into pain that lasts,
Should have knew they were fake,
There's nobody here to trust,

I sit alone every night looking at the stars,
Because it's not so lonely up there like it's here,
Where All I have is these tears and scars,
I'm nothing but a broken glass,

I just feel like a broken glass,
So broken don't know if I'll last,
The shattered pieces from my past,
I'm just a broken glass.

Dear Creator,

Today I feel lost, I feel so useless and helpless. Today I decided that I'll write things down like write about how I am feeling and write about what I go through every day. I know this way it helps me release some pain away from and helps me get things of my mind. I feel like when I write stuff down it gives me a sense of relief from pain and that way I don't have to bear all the weight of the world on my shoulders.

I'm just tired, mentally and physically. I always feel like people don't really care about how I feel and when they look at me they look at me like I'm some sort of an alien or a germ forgetting that I'm just as the same as you a human made of flesh and blood. That may not be the case but to me it seems that way every time. Maybe it's because I always put myself down and maybe it's because in the past the things people have been saying to me, I've started to believe it. Now I can't even stand myself sometimes.

I always felt alone I was too afraid to admit it to the people that love me, in fact I've always been on my own since the very start. I just wanted someone to understand me and how I really feel, understand my pain and not have people telling me that there are other people going through worse than you. What you think I don't already know that?

When I do tell people how I feel the impression I get is like I'm just a sad, depressed, lonely man that needs to grow up. But the funny thing is everyone that I do speak to always tell me I'm such a nice & funny person to be around; they get surprised when they know of my story.

It's so weird because now I can take a step back and see why I went through all of the things I had to go through. This just makes me believe that everything does happen for a reason. I can see why you made me go through all of that and I know you have created me to accomplish many great things in the future.

'I wanted to write, write stories and read, read stories, till I forget mine'

Finding peace within ourselves

If you want to live a peaceful life and you truly want happiness than the only person that will stop you from doing that is yourself. Before you do anything you need to ask yourself what peace means to me and what does living a peaceful life look like to me.

Living a peaceful life to me means living a happy life because if you are happy you are in peace. Peace and happiness may not be the same thing but when you have figured out a way to combine the two and include it to your life then you'll see what I mean. But to get to that level you need to face yourself and I mean you have to go into a full battle with yourself, just you and your inner self.

Some people find that by getting therapy, doing yoga, meditating etc, will help you relax and be at peace and feel that peaceful feeling. And yes I'm not saying I disagree but what I'm saying is that, end of the day it all comes down to you. Who told you that if you get therapy or do yoga and meditation it will help you find peace? Well the answer is simple, you told yourself that by getting all these services you will feel better about yourself and you'll finally feel peaceful. But just think for a second, what if you told yourself that you don't need all these services and that the only reason your feeling the way you're feeling? Is because you made yourself feel that way. You made yourself into an obstacle and a big wall that you cannot overcome.

'If it's not going to matter in 5 years, don't spend more than 5 minutes being upset by it!!'

My mother a true queen

My mother a true queen,

Dropping tears hearing screams,

Peaceful days is what she dreams,

But a tortured reality is what it seems,

She cared for others even when she felt down,

She always smiled you will never see a frown,

Wanted to get away from everything get away from this town,

Even through it all she still held her crown,

A true queen she is the one I always miss,

She rather feed her Child & starves,

That's the type of woman she is,

I used to blame you for leaving me alone,

But as life went on I understood why you was gone,

Trapped in this persona feeling sorry for myself,

But this is an endless cycle stuck in this dome,

I want success and everything in here,

But I don't want any of those things if you are not here,

I only want to do it for you,

But not achieving that is something I used to fear,

But not any more,

Anxiety and depression eating away her brain,

Chronic headaches can't stand the pain,

Nothing ever seems the same,

Everything in this life will always change,

Tired of hearing everyone speaking bad about you,

There was times where I used to think it was true,

My anger didn't let me see past it all,

Now I finally I understand what you had to go through,

The day I saw that man hit you, my innocent eyes
became ruthless,

I prayed god give me strength and patience,

If only I was older I would grab his throat and smash his
head to the floor,

So what if he is my dad,

He has no right to treat a women not even a human in fact,

But I know that is not right,

End of the day he still my dad and my mum taught me better,

So I'll be successful and when I get married I'll show him how you love your wife and kids.

That will be the day he regrets for ever doubting his DNA,

That day will be when he says I'm sorry and I love you?

But it will be too late.

But through it all my mum always used to say,

That all this bad things that are happening to me,

Is because something really good is about to happen to me,

And those lines saved me got me to where I am in life right now,

Every failure every struggle I remembered those words,

And every time things got better and better.

My mum was absolutely right!

Maybe when my mum said that,

She was talking about me,

That I will be that amazing future,

That will come after this bad.

My mother a true queen,

Flashbacks from her past,

Burying the burning tears because never lost hope,

My mother a true queen, holding her crown,

She knows I'm something she is looking forward to,

Fighting battles fighting her cries,

Like a queen she conquers and win,

And just like that she forever ruled the lands!

Dropping tears hearing screams,

Peaceful days is what she dreams,

But a tortured reality is what it seems.

My mother a true queen

My Mother – The Queen

My mother, I don't even know where to start there is so much I can say about my mother. There is nothing more precious in this whole world than you, mum. You come before anything else. I never knew you could sacrifice so much for me. For everything you have been through there is nothing I would not do for you. I'll do anything for you mum. You are the reason for my being. You deserve the best of everything in this world and after that as well.

The look in her eyes, the love in her heart such a queen.

She is pure royalty.

At the age of 19, my mother was made to get married and be part of a family that she had no clue about. Forget that she didn't even get to see the man she was marring till few days before the wedding.

Yes I know exactly what you are thinking, but unfortunately that's how so many people back then got married in our country. To be honest till this day I don't even know the point of that, like was there really a benefit getting married that way or was it just a cultural thing that our ancestors "thought it was right" but it clearly isn't. The really hurtful thing is that this kind of treatment is still happening in our world so that certainly needs to change.

My mother had to leave everything behind all her dreams and especially her education to become a full time wife and a tortured servant for her husband's family.

I gave a long thought about writing this in my book but then I thought you know what? I think it's time everyone should know about this no more hiding it, everyone is going to know how these people treated my mother and why today she a true queen.

My mum would work so hard doing all the house chores and even cooking to only get treated like she is someone with no value someone that's lesser than them. When she served the food to her mother in law she used to just throw the food on the floor under the table right in front of my mother saying the food is disgusting. Her mother in law, my grandma would never eat so she would wake up in the middle of night, turn on all the lights in the house, shouting loudly to herself with evil words cursing everyone.

My dad was always away in another country because he worked abroad so he was never here to witness all this, and my mother didn't have anyone to explain how she was being treated. Even when my dad did come back and stayed he never believed what my mum said he would always take his families side no matter what even if they were in the wrong.

You would think that at least the husband treats his wife good but I'm sorry to say that was not the case here, in fact he treated my mum even worse. He was very controlling, abusive and treated his wife in a manner where she was lower than him in every way. Every time he came back from this other country he worked at he just used to go out to his older sister's house and stay there all day going out and whatever he was doing with them I don't even want to know.

He never got anything for my mother; never did he bring her a gift or take her out somewhere nice.

To him his family was everything, forgetting about his wife and kids. He did more for them than he did for us because we didn't mean anything to him. I'm not just talking about money but love and everything a father package includes. He did more for his sister and his sisters kids than he did for us. He fed them, gave them money every single month, helped them built a house, buy them all these things. You get the point there is way more he did for them than us!

By the time my mother was 21 I was born, I was like a new hope and motivation for my mum to get out of this tortured hell hole. We were so poor that we didn't have enough food for my mum to eat and for her to feed me at the same time. My grandpa and my grandma (my mother's parents) used to send a lot of food to us every few months that kept us going.

As I grew a bit older and started to take my first steps I spent most of my time in my grand parents house. I don't even remember much of my time in my dad's house.

It was an escape for my mum to get away from all that constant drama, fighting and torture from my dad's side. So she always ended up back at grandpa's house with me because she always thought about my well being before anything else, and she didn't want me growing up in that environment.

All this was just emotional and mental abuse for my mum it affected her so much. It affected her mentally and physically. How it affected her mentally? She had regular anxiety attacks, where her heart rate increased rapidly making her breathing heavy and fast, almost feeling as if all of her oxygen, every last breath is being extracted from her forcefully. Trembling and shaking from head to toe as the images of her torture episodes keeps replaying reminding her that there is no freedom.

The anxiety attacks were so bad it made her heart fragile and caused problems where 6 years down the line she will find out that she is in need of a heart surgery otherwise her heart could fail.

Not long after the abuse and after the attacks started, depression had introduced itself to my mum. Depression gave her the tools to stay awake at night making her brain tired every day and making her feel hollow and scared.

Depression has no specific symptoms nor does it have an explanation or a reason for it happening to you. But having said that what I do know is that depression builds up from little pieces of your life that have hurt you, or caused you pain or made you feel like not getting up from bed.

Depression and anxiety made my mother scared and gave her a huge fear of not ever speaking out. They treated her so badly but she couldn't speak up for herself or defend herself and fight against it, instead she used to carry on with her work quietly and tears would just drop.

These tears were off feeling helpless, unwanted,

powerless, broken, damaged, hurt, destroyed, unloved and trapped.

I think she gave up at that time because we lived in a country where everything was corrupt and not everyone there was nice. If she were to go the police they would not do anything because bribing the police was so easy, it was easy as giving a kid some sweets to forget about why he/she is crying in the first place.

No one would help and no one did help my mum. I was her new reason to fight and I was and I am! Her hope for her peace, justice, happiness and freedom!

Her silent tears would not stop and her desperate calling for help in her prayers would not stop. She would pray to GOD saying to make me, her son, someone really big, someone successful, someone that is motivated, someone that is a true revolutionist and someone that will stand up for people like her. She prayed to god that he never make me like my dad or anyone from his family, that god makes me a better person and make me into someone that will bring change to the world.

It wasn't long before god answered her prayers and when I was 6, after my mum and dad had their fight and after witnessing my dad hit my mum I went to my grandpa and told him everything, told him what my mother couldn't say all these years.

After seeing my dad hit my mum, after seeing him treat a women in this manner was the first ever lesson I learnt in my life at the age of 6. I know exactly how my mum felt how it affected her even with her depression and anxiety. How do you think I know all this so well and how I described it so well and almost too perfectly? It's because I have suffered from anxiety and depression too and it was on that day that it left its mark on me. I mean come on an innocent child should never ever have to witness that horror and torture, leaving nothing but a scarred image that will soon come to haunt later down the line.

I knew that one day all this was going to make me really successful.

After telling my grandpa everything he immediately got me, my mum and my little sister out of that house. I thought that this will be the end of the torture my mum had to face but I was wrong this was something that will haunt her for many years to come. Little did I know that this was also going to haunt me for the rest of my life?

After a while I had to leave my mother to come to London at the age of 7. I had no idea why but all I knew that this was the biggest sacrifice my mother had ever made. I'm still finding about this but what I have told you so far is all the information I have gathered over the years.

Mum you raised me and my little sister while being dragged into the underworld. You raised two kids while being tortured, sacrificed everything so we can be healthy. You put others first and always helped them even though you was the one in need of help. Mum you are a true revolutionist and you taught me not to take shit from anyone. I watched you from young and saw how you strong you really are. You was sitting on the throne way before you became a true queen. Mum you went through so much and still managed to show love to people, you even tried to give us everything. Through all this mum one thing you didn't realise is that I was watching all this time and you just gave birth to someone that will follow your steps. Even before I was born you was going through way more that I can imagine what it was like then. Through it all I learnt the lessons of life way before I knew what life was about. The words you taught me and the examples I witnessed first hand, have made me a fighter, believer, lover, helper and a world changer. Powerful and strong with no fear but the fear of my creator. Unstoppable motivation that will never die. Mum you taught me that and you showed me what life should be like. You did all of that while chains holding you down, burning your skin till it bleeds. That is how it felt like right. Mum tell me how you did. Wow. I'm so happy I am your son and I am so happy that I am on this mission that you couldn't complete.

My mother is the most inspirational person to me till this day. A role model I will never be able to be like but I know for sure I will be like that person she prayed for because our creator will never reject a prayer of a soft, loving, caring and an innocent mother!

'Being alone is a power very few can handle'

Piano Keys

It's like piano keys
Every struggle plays different notes,
Every sound and every feel
It's a different mode,

The mode I never prepared for,
Life takes you at a surprise,
A face expression
That shows no despise,

Wondering where I would end up next,
People come and go so who will be next,
Trying to fix everything around me
But I just end up a mess and a wreck,

I did good with all the bad I had,
But somehow I still feel
There is something missing,

I tried being a gentleman
But the man inside
Didn't want to be that gentle,
I'm just watching everything around me
Fall and crumble,
Making me go crazy and mental,

I guess I can't quit
Till I'm living the life
I dream about,
Until the cells in my body
Move as one with every melody,

It's like piano keys,
Sometimes you feel like
Playing something magical,
And Sometimes you just want revenge,

Its like piano keys
I can't explain,
I can hear a different song
Each Time playing in my head,
It calms down my psychosis
And does not make me go insane,

(sigh)…piano keys
You see it's these piano keys.

Positive mind-set

You know sometimes I feel a certain way and sometimes I don't really understand people. There are days I wake up feeling all these negative emotions and everything just hits you like a big wave. You start thinking about how you keep failing, how things are no changing and how the female you wanted to be with does not want to be with you.

What heartbreak and a let-down right? Especially that last one that one stings. Hurts for a long time trust me. But anyway there are some emotions that hurt more than others and that will last longer if you let it.

In order to stay positive you have to be negative because the two cannot exist without the other one, just like love can't exist without hate. Do you agree?

I think positivity is all about acceptance. You need to accept all negative side to yourself. Accept all your flaws and imperfections realise that you're not perfect, you will make mistakes, and you will have obstacles you need to overcome and that you can't stop these negative thoughts that annoy you all the time.

People always say to me to let go of the past, but how

can I let go of all the pain I've felt, all the experiences I had and all the feelings of different emotions I've felt. I'll never forget them even if I become the most happiest man in the world because my past is who I am and it's what made me who I am today.

Sometimes I think if I was to die right now would I be happy with myself or would I just be laying there on my last breath wondering if people will miss me, would they cry for me, would they know of all the things I had to go through, would they appreciate me for who I was, would they remember me, would they talk about me, would they talk about how I was and what kind of a person I was?

Did I really have an impact on people's lives? Did I really motivate and inspire others? Did I really do anything to change people's lives?

Maybe God just decided that this is far as I go, I've done enough, I've done my bit and now it's time to finally join him and be with him, so I can just sit with him and tell him all the stories of my life and just sit there beside my creator and drop my tears.

The best thing about that is that God already knows what I've been through but he would still listen to me tell my tale, and when I can't say any more my tears will just fall and he will understand every reason for those tears every single drop he'll understand without me even saying anything.

'The world is full of good people, if you can't find one be one'.

If you want something just chase it, pursue it. No matter how hard it is no matter how much it hurts. This place is unfair and sometimes you can't have what you want, I know that really hurts. Accept it, make it a part of you, and use it as your fuel. You fuel your motivation, hunger and determination. Use that to show and prove why you deserve it more than anyone else.

People are going to laugh, tell you it's not a good idea, look down on you, pay no attention to you; they won't respect you, appreciate you or not even value you. But that's just makes it more of a reason why you must do it and most Important for yourself. Why worry about what people have to say any ways end of the day it is your life not theirs. You should always do what you think is right. Yes that means going to university because you want to, not because your mum or dad said you should go. You should always focus on what makes you satisfied and how you pictured living the rest of the days.

If today was the last day you will be alive, how would you spend this last day?

Imagine just knowing this thought how everyone will start panicking trying to figure out what is the one thing that they love. Or what is the one thing that is important to them more than anything else. But see how it is easy to forget this when we live it every day of our lives not knowing that today could be the last. Every day we have a chance to do what we love and focus on what the most important things are in our life. Unfortunately most people are living a life according to what is most important to them. Most people will procrastinate and leave the things they love the most to when they are more stable etc. whatever that is supposed to mean. Stable? Good joke. Life is not stable and neither are your goals. Meaning you can't be living waiting for things to be perfect or waiting for the perfect time. If you want to travel the world like I how I want to then work hard make some money and go. I have a whole list of places written down that I would like to travel to one day and I will.

New Horizon Youth Centre

I used to attend a youth centre based in Euston, London. When I attended this centre I've met a lot of people, young individuals like myself. Everyone that attended was/is homeless or had terrible experiences and events happening in their lives.

It really shocked me and hurt me to see so many young, smart individuals stuck and trapped in this horrifying and heart breaking situation.

Like this is London I didn't know things like this happen here.

I realised that I wasn't the only one that was homeless and had so much problems in their lives. I started talking to them and the stories they told me and what they had to go through really got to me and really hurt me.

If you ever go to an old peoples care home and you start talking to them. When you see the regret in their eyes it really gets to you. The dreams, ideas and inventions they had that never got the chance to happen it really makes you think and really makes you get up off your backside and chase your goals.

And then you compare it to the young kids that are homeless you see the hunger for success in their eyes but unfortunately because of the circumstances, no help or an opportunity they can't achieve their goals in life. That's not fair.

I began to wonder and question, why life is like this. Why do some people deserve to live a luxury life while others are suffering? Why do some people have 5-6 bedrooms when there is someone with no roof over their head. Why does someone else deserve to live like a king or a queen?

Is it because they have more money, because they look

better, dress better, speak better or they are better humans?

I think not in fact I know they not cause we all equal right? Yeah right!! Heard that many times but when it comes down to humanity we are all lost. Lost souls, selfish, it's always give, give, give me, not here let me give, give, give to someone or let me help, help, help someone.

I feel for my people it gets to me all the time. I guess this is just how I am this is just how I am this is the type of person my creator has made me into and I don't think I'll ever change even if I want to because my heart always takes me back to the people to being to the people to being who I really am. That is my strength, my strongest most powerful part that I am most thankful and love about myself.

And I think that is the realist it can get. I've always thought about creating a system where it helps people on a much larger scale where it can completely change someone's life.

THAT'S EXACTLY WHAT I AM GOING TO DO!!

'TALK ABOUT A BAD DAY I LIVE A LIFE LIKE THAT'.

Would you

Tell me would you die for me,

Tell me would you ride for me,

Would you defend me when they lie about me?

Or will you make excuses & just walk away.

Tell me would you appreciate my struggles,

Tell me would you listen to me talk,

Tell me would you love like no other,

Would you understand me even if I say nothing?

Tell me would you love me even if I had nothing,

Would you still hug me even if I wore torn out clothes,

Tell me will you just play mind games with me,

Or would you sit and talk to me and be real,

Tell me would you love me for who I am and not what you want me to be,

Would you stay up with me & talk about all the things life put us through,

Would you drop everything just to be with me?

Tell me would you want me to treat you right,

Or would you want me to chase you like a little boy,

Tell me would you be a woman and be by my side,

Would you be with me every step of the way when things

get hard,

when there are strong tides?

Don't ever hurt me or lie to me,

Tell me straight up what I mean to you,

Tell me if you want to be with me or not,

No more games no more drama,

Tell me that you'll pull me out of this darkness I'm stuck in,

tell me would you want to travel and build our empire with me,

Tell me that everything you just read? Made you cry,

Tell me that you want to be everything I mentioned, tell me you love my pains, because it made me love you,

So tell me would you want to be with a man like me.

The Biggest Failure

So many successful people say that without failure there is no success. To me, the way I see it is that there are no clear paths to walk every path you take has something challenging that you have to overcome. A path of failures is a path of success.

I've always been a failure. I keep repeating myself and that's because it's just that important to me.

I've failed over and over again at everything. There have been people in my life that have told me that I am a failure and made me actually believe for a while that I was.

When things just don't go your way, when all you want to do is make people proud of you and you just feel like no matter what you do that does not happen.

Failure is my fuel. I use my failures, my setbacks and my struggles as my motivation to get out of bed in early and work on my dream. Most people just give up after trying few times and they settle for what they have.

Sometimes it's hard to wake up in the morning; mind full of demons pulling you down with negative energy feeding you with that there is no point trying any more.

There is no insurance for your broken part, when you are in pain and damaged you have to fix yourself.

Tell me a peaceful place where I can go so I can clear my head and take a break. I tried everything but I'm left with nothing. I'm watching everything fall apart no matter how hard I try I can't hold on to it. It's like holding onto a hot coal. So I let go broke the system now I got a light that's different from everyone else.

Now people can see what separates me from the average.

'Don't expect them to understand your hustle, when they don't have your vision'.

A lot of people especially the younger generation just want it the easy way! They want to be spoon fed and expect it to be done for them.

You are not ready to be alone at night working on your dream, you are not ready to stay awake until am or 4 am in the morning working everyday. You want something? Ask yourself did I put in enough work? Did I really give it my all?

What did you have to sacrifice, what did you have to give up, what struggle did you have to go through that no one else knows about but yourself.

Think of the biggest disadvantages and weaknesses you have. Let me tell you something it's none of those, it's YOU!!

I had so many regrets writing this book because this book will show the side to me that no one sees or knows, these are thoughts, wisdom, knowledge, experience and struggles that only my mind, soul and my creator know about.

But the thing is I know I'm in control, I'm not going to care about what people think about me or what they will see me as because I'm in control because I know I'm unstoppable and after all this I know people still won't understand. They will just go back to living their usual life.

So I might look like or sound like a fool but I know this book will change so many lives, even if it's one person where they wake up in the morning looking forward to the day or they carry on chasing their dreams after giving up that's more than enough for me.

The best motivational speeches that I've heard came from people. When people tell you, you can't do it!! It just makes you want to do it more and prove them wrong. I'll show you, I'll show you what I can do!!

Just because you have failed once don't mean you are a failure. It just takes one time!! ONE TIME!! To get it right and then you are set, you just have to keep trying till that one time embraces you like a big tornado hitting and this time you are ready more than ever.

Have you ever went out to try to do something, something

different and you come home, you know that you didn't give it your all that there was much more you could have done. But you didn't want to look ugly or look silly because your girlfriend was watching you or your boys were there, so you held back. Now you have all these regrets because you know that you are ten times better than how people actually see you as.

Wake up tomorrow and do something different, and understand that if you do the same thing as today? Then you are STUCK. Just because you did something a certain way yesterday don't mean you have to do it that way today.

If you can't push your limitations and ideology? what is the point? If there was a rule that says that certain people have more boundaries than you? then that's understandable. BUT it's not!! We all have the same chances to push and work hard.

We all have the same 24 hours in a day. So there are no excuses!!

Like Malcom X said Do whatever is necessary!!

Apologies if I've misinterpreted that but you get the point.

Rejections after rejections after rejections, how many more times do I have to listen to people say they want nothing to do with me they don't want to hear my ideas, they don't want to know the person I am. How many times do I have to sit there and have you tell me that it's going to be okay when I know it ain't, because I'm still here trapped in the same place? One thing I'm looking forward to is proving all these people wrong, it's an opportunity they have missed out on. You should have invested in me when you had the chance. Now watch me win in the most humble and modest way.

Dream Box

Been stuck here for a while,

Running more than a mile,

Asking myself if I'm really alive,

Barely have enough to survive,

Do you know about no plates and an empty dish,

Do you know about living in a room

with just a bed and a fridge,

Do you know about struggling with money

when your life is a mess,

Do you know about people who cry

when there is no laughter left,

Do you know about

being lonely and loosing friends,

Do you know about broken relationships

when there is no love left,

Do you know about goals

when you lose all belief in it,

And do you know about dreams

that live in a box that just suffocate,

Why is it when you have money

people want to take advice from you more?

But if I was broke then

they won't even give a second thought,

Why is it when you look good

people pay attention more?

But if I looked ugly then

they won't even give a second thought,

Why is it when you are famous

people look up to you more?

Now I'm stuck in this box because

my life meant nothing at all,

Looking for opportunities

but can't find the right door,

Rejected from everything

because I looked poor,

So now you have to dress a certain way

and look a certain way to get applause,

No matter how hard I try

I always get ignored,

But you rather watch a silly memes

then someone who has something to fight for,

The world we live in today

does not care about you any more,

And you won't ever be noticed

no matter where you go,

Now everyone walking around

with hearts that are cold and sore,

I had dreams but not any more,

Now I'm stuck in this box

because my life meant nothing at all,

I'm hungry for success

that is something I cannot resist,

But you don't want to give me a chance,

Maybe it's because

my second name is Ahmed

and you think I'm a terrorist?

I have been persistent and consistent,

I don't have all the skills to match your expectations?

Now what kind of nonsense is this?

You tell us not to judge or stereotype,

But you are the most stereotypical one here every time
you type,

Everyone will listen to you because you wear a suit or tie,

Or because you are rich and famous and you are living
the good life,

And you forget about the ones, who are struggling to
survive,

We all had dreams just like you and I,

If only I could be heard that's all I think at times,

A cute cat video will get over 50,000 likes,

It's so sad I would probably get 2 if I just died,

See how the world is messed up right,

Knife to my chest about to commit suicide,

But my dreams remained in a box,

Now I'm taking it with me to the other side.

Suicidal Ideology

The raging heat in my body, the drilling mechanism in my brain, drilling away in my brain taking no notice of the fragile brain cells that hold key information and a step by step manual to operating this vehicle. The constant stabbing and piercing of this migraine that spread through my temple.

The poisonous pain begins to take over other territories in my mind including my eyes.

My eyes have become the victim to this venomous discomfort where it has made these tears discolour from red to dark black.

Making my image in the other dimension, look like a serial killer.

Sitting through therapy listening to them talk like they know how I feel like please, you don't know the places my mind visits every day, you are not GOD to know what's in my heart.

You don't know them nights where you feel so helpless and all you can do is lie in bed and stare at the ceiling in the dark.

I should just slit my wrist, hold my breath or bite my tongue and end this. I'm sick of talking, I'm sick of people lying to me, I'm sick of seeing people pretending like they all happy, like they all that. Come back down to Earth you are just another human made from the dirt, humble yourself.

I'm a failure I'm a good for nothing dumb depressed creation. I wasn't able to make myself into someone big someone that can make a difference someone people can look up to. I'm still that abandoned little boy on the doorstep waiting for his mum to come and show a better way out.

I hate people that have negative feedbacks for me because I've heard them all my life and don't want to hear them any more. If you don't like something about me or what I do or who I am you are more than welcome to go.

I hate when people tell me that I'm doing this wrong and this wrong, that maybe I should be more like this and like that, I should do that and do this.

I don't like being told what to do because I've never had anyone there for me to show me how to survive and live so why now?

You was not there for me when I needed someone most, so don't come here now like you know what's good.

The reason why I'm writing all this is because there were times when I had thoughts like what you have just read, and it's not just me there are way more people out there that have thoughts such as these because of the situations they have been through in life. But I think this is what makes them the strongest and this certainly gives me motivation and hunger to do more and achieve success.

I'm tired, every day is a struggle, every day I have to fight, tired of living a lie, I know I am not normal but I have to fake it, either I pull the trigger on them or I'm left down here begging.

Every time I write I have to fight, because I have to make sure they hear me. This is my path I didn't choose this it is destiny.

All these people have to be someone they are not, they are not happy with the life they are living but yet they choose to live with chains and shackles.

I'm going to get it and there is no stopping it, I wished for death but still did not give in, you fantasise about a dream you want but scared to change the reality you live in.

I want my words to be powerful to be meaningful, so someone can stand up and say I want to change without fearing the unknown. Needed someone to hug me, needed someone to love me, needed the world to be with me, but I ended up being cold and got treated like a disease,
I'm waiting for the day when everybody apologises, but by then it will be too late,

I would have already gone beyond that level to accept anything,
Even the friends you had from day 1, will turn around and name all the favours they did for you, they will say the problem is not them it's you, after all you will think that they will be the ones to understand you the most, but when it comes down to it that concept will be lost,

I Remember when, it took years to create a relationship, but only a second to ruin them, Guess it's true you don't really know someone, until you go against them,

It's good it's all motivation for me, the day I lost my friends is the day I became a Better man, with nothing to lose I became a more successful man,

It's a shame that they didn't get to stay with me through this journey, I had so much plans for them, but people don't want to see visions any more they just want to see money,

I'm only a step away from my success,

Failure

Feeling like a failure,

Feeling like a clone,

You haven't seen what I seen,

You haven't known what I known,

First of all let me start from the heart,

I'm a hustler man,

You were giving me my start,

I know what it's like to wake up feeling messed up, when you been through it all and you just had enough,

All you have is these pains and sorrow,

It's sad when you wish you don't wake up tomorrow,

Suicidal ideologies,

All these people hurt me still no apologies,

If I had another chance I would study astronomy,

But a happy childhood wasn't written for me,

Age 5 left on a woman's doorstep,

Can't remember where it is, where happiness is kept,

No parents around to get me out of this mess,

I had to starve some nights, till the hunger spread to my chest,

Feeling like a failure,

Feeling like a clone,

You haven't seen what I seen,

You haven't known what I known,

Rejections & fake love is all I'm ever shown,

You are not going to make it, if you are afraid to be alone,

It's not my exterior,

It's my soul,

So take note because this is what I own,

Mitak, speak your mind Just let it out,

Told me I will never big,

Let them know what I'm about,

Watch me fly, if you are still having doubts,

I soak in the water like I'm a drought,

Be careful what you say to me watch your mouth,

I don't care where you are from whether it's north or south,

I didn't want to do this but it's on now,

Nothing but Selfish souls, I'll say what I want because I can,

All this makes me angry like I want to rip your head off and revolutionise this land!!!

Feeling like a failure,

Feeling like a clone,

You haven't seen what I seen,

You haven't known what I known,

Where I am in my life right now- 2017

I've been jobless for nearly a year. Rejected from 234 jobs I have applied for. In the process of doing my own thing and starting my own business because I've had enough of working for someone else and making their dreams come true.

So I said you know what I've had enough forget this I'm going to work for myself and make sure that these so called companies that only judge you on what skills you have and they all say that they treat employees "like" family. Last time I checked you don't get to choose what child you have based on what skills and qualities they have. You just love them no matter.

Just like that I want to build a company where everyone can share their ideas you don't have to be a senior or a manager. Where the employees don't feel like employees more like CEO's, where their ideas will be appreciated and they will be trusted to bring what they want to the table and better the company. You will feel like it is your own company, your own business. I want to give everyone the chance to start their own business.

I have recently started my own business where it is split into different parts, such as the charity campaign part, the media part and the mentoring and coaching part.

There is so much more to it but let's not get into that now.

I am also hoping to complete and publish this book soon and then write a part two as well.

Everybody wants to be happy; everybody wants to feel

happiness that's one goal everyone has in common.

Waving

I dream of waves,
I dream of the ocean,
I dream about what life is like when you have freedom.

Walls and walls, conceal my brain,
For you not know what is outside this frame,

It's like living with no air but having patience,
now how does that work
because without the other one is none existent,

I'm so busy in this world,
that I have forgotten what I love & who loves me,
What I need & what makes me breathe,
What really matters & how to dream,

I have forgotten myself by this selfishness,
I've only realised this after I have poisoned myself,

I have forgotten the visions and the ideologies,
that got me excited as a kid,
because the worst place you could be is looking at
yourself with apologies,

I dream of waves,
I dream of the ocean,
I dream about what life is like when you have freedom.

Working hard or working smart?

It's not about working hard and working late, it's about
creating your future as long as you are working on your
dreams, your goals every day, and you are currently in
the process of creating the future you want! This means
every spare time you get your working, when you come
back from your nine to five job working, make it a full
time hobby if that's what it takes, but no matter what you
can't stop working on your future, no excuses, no
procrastinating. This does not mean you are doing

something you don't like no, it means you are working on something you love doing something that makes you happy. That's exactly what I do I found what I enjoy, what I love, what makes me happy and just found a way to do that for a living.

If you just like to sit there all day and watch movies? That's fine; now find a way to make money from doing that. Sounds crazy right I know but that kind of thinking is why most people nowadays are not doing what makes them happy. Everything has possibilities and everything has a way. We as humans don't have any restrictions to how far minds can travel so why do you put restrictions on your beliefs? Trust in yourself and believe that you can make it happen. The only thing that will stop you is you. So decide now!

Simply by writing I've been blessed. I started off with the intention of changing the world but as life went on and as I kept on failing, God showed me that I can't change what he has already written. So now the least I can do is make it easy for everyone, by educating the right and helping each other.

Dear my people stuck in poverty, to all those who are

stereotyped to something we are not. To those who are victims of fascism and victims of this secret racist society. The only difference there is to how it was in the old times to how it is now? Is that before there were all these problems and we all knew it and now there is still all these problems but it's just portrayed in a beautiful way and kept a secret, an illusion of your own destruction and struggle.

I started as a selfish energy that just wanted to be rich and on top so I can live a lazy life. But now my purpose has completely changed and my view on what it means to be successful has also changed. Now I'm an antidote for the world a cure for the world. Either it will be me physically making a difference, or the work I will leave behind, or the people that will be inspired and carry on even long after I'm gone.

There were days I just wanted to be with god, I prayed to just be with him. Death was something I didn't mind at all. But I always knew it wasn't my time yet to go, I have a lot to do before I go, before it's my time to meet my creator.

I always felt like my creator had something special just for me and he made me go through what I did in order to achieve that speciality. Now everything that I'm doing is a step closer to that.

There was a time I just sit there and watch the world. I start thinking, all of a sudden I have so many ideas and start seeing all these possibilities that I never saw before.

So many people are distracted and kept busy with other things that they forget about what they truly want. Phone and technology is one of those tools that distract us. There is so much talent and brilliant ideas out there but they are restricted from the distractions we are involved with.

How to create a successful company & business!

* Building Relationships
* Building good lasting relationships with everyone is one key part to what makes someone really successful especially if you want to build a company and start your own business.
* Having a successful business means having a successful relation with your employees.
* Most people fail with their employees

because they say they will treat them "like" a family when what you should be doing is making sure that all your employees are a family.

* Everyone should feel like they have a value here and everyone should be able to feel like they are part of something.

* You put customers first when you fail to understand that most important thing is your employees.

* When employee can come into work and they can share ideas and actually take part leading your company you will see that the employees will give it there all and it will no longer be working for someone else feel like it's their own business.

* You have fun and you don't make them feel like you are the one on top and they are someone lower than you.

* Making them feel equal and treating them well helps and comes a long way.

* Your employees look forward to work and feel like all the opportunities are right at their hands.

* Building good relationships is not just with

your employees but with your clients, customers and everyone else you meet.

* You always have to leave a good impression and you always have to make sure that everyone you meet can take something from you and you can take something from them.

* A perfect example is, after the meeting leave them a short snappy nice email. 'Hi John hope you are well, it was a pleasure meeting you today really appreciate the time. Please let me know if you would like to meet again or if you have any ideas that we can work on I'll be delighted to help, thanks. Kind regards your name' etc.

* You'll see after this nice pleasing email it will open doors of opportunities and help you keep this good relationship.

* This does not just improve relationships between you and your employee but when they go home they will treat their spouses and children better because they had a good day at work and the spouses and children will treat whoever they know better.

* You just created a chain of good, lasting

and healthy relationships.

When you have child you don't choose them saying oh I want the child to have green eyes, curly brown hair, smart etc. So why do we use this same exact method to choose our employees. Oh we are looking for someone that is diverse qualified, 5 years experience etc. Then you have these employers saying here in our company we are like a family and make everyone feel like a family. Oh please come on who are you trying to fool.

With these two faced fake companies it's only about one thing that's numbers and being at the top that's it. You want to be at the top and want numbers and then what. Why are you doing what you are doing?

Everyone acts like they got it all figured out and they know exactly what they are doing. But when asked what is your main goal? What is your purpose? Or why are you doing this? You are unable to give a flawless answer.

I'm afraid the answers are not good enough. In fact it just sounds too fake and selfish. Like you are showing you the good guy while playing the bad guy.

We are good at showing people that life is great. So when you ask what should we do? And all the senior people that think that they got all figured out and know everything, say this is what you have to do. And they have no clue.

I feel like I'm stuck still struggling going through failures and I know that's always going to be there but I want to be doing something I enjoy and love sometimes I forget I'm only 19 but still feels like I'm running out of time and I need to do something with my life.

'Having a good healthy routine not only gives you a lot of health benefits, but also the chance to create some healthy relationships and make good decisions in life.'

I don't like it when people say "you work for me" I completely disregard this saying and idea.

'You shouldn't throw glass at your glass house, it will break & you shouldn't throw water at your mud house, it will melt away everything, making it weak.'

My foster parents

I was 16 or 17 I think can't quite remember when I came
into care. I had social workers visiting me when I was little
after 2010 they stopped didn't visit any more. I guess they
probably saw I was okay and didn't need the support, I
don't know.

I came into care not knowing where I'll be or what I will be
doing with my life. Everything was a mess. At first social
workers were being really hard and wasn't taking me in
as I had nowhere to go.

 I got in touch with an organisation called Coram Voice.
They help young people's voices be heard. I had an
advocate that helped me a lot. She got me in touch with a
solicitor that challenged the care system to take me in.
After two or three months she managed to get the social
workers to finally take me in. As I was under 18 and it's
unlawful to keep a minor out on the streets. That's when I

met my foster parents. I was given my own room to stay in and they helped me get myself back on my feet. I was going through a lot. At the time I had dropped out of school and the job I was working at too. My mind was confused and lost in so many places I couldn't even explain. I gave up with everything felt like there is no point trying I always end up starting over again and nothing goes the way I want it to. But somehow I still had that little bit of hunger to do better and be successful. Somehow I still knew what I really wanted in life. But I also knew that I need to fix myself before I can go ahead and do that. There are few things I need come to terms with and there are few issues I need to solve first. Like how I did I end up in these situations and how can I deal with these mental issues. At first I hated being there in my foster parent's house. I felt really out of place because it was strangers that I met today and I have to live with them for the next few months.

I knew that I need to focus on myself first make sure I'm good before I do anything else. My foster parents played a big part in helping me. Before I knew it I got my routine back to normal, I was eating properly and sleeping properly. I felt safe like I didn't have to worry about being out on the street again or worry about how I'm going to survive without any money. They gave me such words of wisdom about life. They showed me what a family should be like. Even their son he is like an older brother to me he helped in every way and was always there for me. Even now that I moved out to my own place he still calls me and checks up on me if I need anything if I'm good.

After 2 or 3 months while I was staying there, another two little boys joined me. They also had their room. They are brothers so they shared a room. They were both still at primary school. I ended up building such a good relationship with them two. I would enjoy spending time with them and get to play with them. We had football sessions every Saturday, few of the neighbours and the kids in the local area would attend and we would have a really good game of football. My health improved hugely and I was always looking forward to a Saturday. During my time that I was staying at my foster parent's house I mostly stayed at home. I guess I was just taking my time to just relax and get my head straight. I was in a process of becoming the best version of myself, even till this day

I'm still working on being just that.

I would do volunteer work with the local borough and the social care team. Working with young individuals like me that is in care. It really helped me get myself out there more and realise that it's not just me there are way more people out there going through worse situations.

One of the moments I remember most was when my foster parents would encourage the two little ones to keep with their routines. Meaning after school you can play for an hour, study or revise for a bit, have a bath by seven, eat dinner and eight O clock you are in bed. They would read and then go sleep to wake up nice and early ready for the next day. This was perfect to me! It was just what I needed and what I was missing. Especially because I felt like everything was all over the place. I knew then that yes I need to have a routine like that. It motivated me so much that I started to discipline myself.

I became way stricter with myself and started to set goals. Set goals to improving myself and then start to work on my goals to become successful. Back then I thought about success but it was all about having money, now when I think about success, it is about the amount of happiness and contentment I have in my life. Being able to breathe freely and not worry about things that don't really matter. I thought about working a normal job, I hated that idea. It just wasn't in my nature to work a 9 to 5 I just couldn't do it. I said to myself, is this how I want the rest of my life to be like? Every day is the same thing. Just living to work a job I don't enjoy? No I can't, I want something better I mean I deserve way more.

My foster parents helped me a lot, the time I spent at that house with them have helped me develop myself. I thank them for everything they have done. I'll remember it for the rest of my life. I still go and visit them although I haven't been in a while I definitely need to go again and see them.

There are some people in this world that truly care about you. Just don't let them go, keep them in your life. It is hard nowadays to find people like that, you would be lucky enough to even get a smile from someone walking past you on the streets. Let alone a quick conversation. Society has divided us so bad that we no longer see any benefit in helping or going out your way to talk to someone that may need your expertise. Even if they don't we as humans need communication otherwise we feel lost and become depressed. Lonely too. Everyone is so moody and just keeping to themselves. The only time you see anything fun, funny or entertaining is on the internet. Well it is known as social media now. But when you come back to reality and back it the real life everyone is so serious and so selfish.

If people don't see any sort of benefit from interacting with you, I am sorry to say they won't interact. Instead they give you that who the hell are you and what are you doing here energy.

There are some of us who are helping people and who are doing what humans should be doing. However it is not enough! We don't need any more musicians, rappers, singers, entertainers, actors, politicians or any selfish beings. We need more thinkers, world changers, helpers, inventors, scientists, I didn't want to use this word because it is being used lightly in our world today, "entrepreneur" but yes we need more of that too. We need people that are less selfish and that are willing to make a difference to other people's lives without expecting anything in return. Like why can't we all just live together without all these rules, regulations, trust issues and without the mentality of, this is mine get out of my way and I don't care what happens to you because that's not my problem.

There is a lot people who fake it, they say they are entrepreneur but when you do some research on them, you soon find out they are nothing but pony fakers. It makes me mad because that means for those that are real out there people like me that are trying to make real difference, we don't get that much chances as the so Called fakers ruined it for us.

All your fault

I'm so tired,

For all the problems you have been causing me,

I'm falling, I'm falling'

It's all your fault,

It's funny when your little

They tell you that you can be whatever you want to be,

And when you want to stand on your own feet,

They will be the first to cut your legs with a saw

Straight through your bone marrow,

Goddamn…

Too many people judging my life,

Too many racist bigots,

That tell you because your not white

You can't be anything,

I'm so tired

I mean like emotionally & mentally,

For all the problems you have been causing me

I hope you burn in hell,

Slowly & dramatically,

Where is god, where is death

And where is Satan,

No one was here when I needed it,

This pain feels like I chewed on a knife

And swallowed all the pieces,

Cutting all my organs on its way down,

I want to throw up,

So I cut my skin open

And go topless,

We are not cool no more,

So don't show me your face

And get lost with your toxic tongue,

You twisted hypocritical female dog,

Stop taking credit for things you have never done,

Stop making it out

Like you did a lot for me,

I hate your guts,

Your the type of woman that makes me vomit,

It's all your fault,

Your torture made me this crazy,

Your torture makes me feel like

Feeding you your own brain,

Because I don't know what you was thinking,

Maybe you should swim in your own blood

Go ahead you two faced crippled witch start sinking,

Now I can't get these thoughts out of my head,

I would laugh & have a drink with you,

And at the same time plan your death,

Just in case you ever decide to spit in my face

And I'm here broken once more,

Emotional blackmail,

I told you I'll never forget

No matter where I be,

You thought you was the monster

Wait till you see what I have in store for you,

More money, More problems,

More love, More hatred,

I'm dead, I'm gone,

So is my love

It will never come back,

I'm so tired,

For all the problems you have been causing me,

I'm falling, I'm falling,

It's all your fault.

They told me I have to be someone else

When I was looking for new opportunities and wanted to start a business and look for partners or investors or even clients. There were some others out there that told me I have to be someone else in order to progress and move forward. I remember one of them told me I have to be "white" whatever that's supposed to mean. "You have to act white" meaning in other words if you are not white chances are you are not going to get anything. I have to dress a certain way and talk a certain way. I remember someone even saying to me to take out my second name 'Ahmed' when I'm emailing potential clients. I was so disgusted and I was so angry. I didn't even know what to say at that time or even what to think. Even when I was pitching any new projects I wanted to start, people would straight away try to make it their own. By saying I should take this part out and should do this instead. People are not going to like this idea maybe try this way.

They straight away shut you out and they say things like there is no market for this, it's going to be hard, there is a lot of competition etc. These types of people let just say they don't like to try anything new. Because of them they made me feel like I had no chance of becoming successful.

I knew this is not the way I will never be someone I'm not. I rather die than let the world change me.

I'm always going to be real and do what's right. Even if I was offered millions for a project but I have to be someone else to get that? No way will I never accept that. Everything that I will be doing will be the way I want and will be in the truest form. I don't need to change my ideas I will keep my ideas as it is. They might not like what I have to offer them. I know there is someone out there that will appreciate my innovations for the future and my ideas to bring change to the world.

I will always be myself and I will carry on with what I have set out to achieve. I am weird and I am different. I am that boy that once sat on the street thinking about a future full of success. Forget about my colour and forget about my name, don't just read these words but understand what I am saying. Stop this stereotype and stop this persona that was created by fools. Just because I don't have a fancy car or wearing a suit and tie it does not mean I am not successful. Stop judging someone before you got to know what they are about and let people be themselves because that's what makes us, us.

The world we live in today.

There are elements of truth and there are elements of falsehood. In today's world we are told that if we do this and do that we can achieve what we want. We are told that we will attract certain things because of the way we are. So in other words if we get robbed, or raped or bullied or discriminated it is because of the way we are and that's what we attracted? That does not make any sense to me.

No, it's not because we attracted those things that it happened to us. It is because unfortunately there are some people who are cold hearted people, that have the heart to do that to another human being.

Then you have these people that tell you, stay positive, be motivated, be successful and achieve your dreams etc.

Don't get me wrong I tell these people the same thing but my reason and purpose for saying these things is on a different level from them.

Just ask yourself, for what reason are you doing all this for? Are you doing it to be rich and famous? Is it so you can have lots of money, cars, and a big mansion?

If your doing all of this to have these materialistic objects that give you temporary happiness and pleasure, then your telling everyone that you have no self esteem, your not happy with your life and your not happy with who you are! You need these objects to feel better about yourself.

Now let's not romanticise poverty, we all know how hard it is coming from a background where we have no choice but to chase money just to survive and put food on our plate, and it's not your fault that you are poor and have to work so hard for your natural human right to survive. You have to work so hard for your natural human needs, just to eat and live.

Shouldn't that be our right anyway? FOR FREE!

I'm entitled to eat because that is a necessity it is something I need otherwise I die. You want a TV, a car? Go work for that because that's something we want, not need, we don't need that we can live without that, but food and shelter? Hmm I think not!

It's like saying hey you! You do this for me and I'll let you eat and live and if you don't then you can just suffer and die because i'll just get someone else tomorrow. I don't really care it don't matter to me I still get to eat!!

It's time everyone wakes up and realise that this is the the capitalistic system we are living in. If this isn't slavery then I don't know what is.

Let's face it there isn't a place for everyone in a society like this, a society that runs on inherited privileges. People that are making it don't prove anything does not prove the system works. The majority people who play by the rules don't make it, because we live in a society that it can't be fulfilled no matter how hard you try.

Only the rich benefit from a society that is only made for the middle class. A perfect example of this is that when we have exams at school, the language the questions are set out is exactly the way middle class people speak. Since little you were taught to speak in that manner. On the other hand working class people don't speak that posh or formal language in their everyday life so you can already imagine the level we are talking here. Now I'll leave the rest for you to find out.

You might agree with me or disagree with me, but regardless this is just how I see the world and this is what I've learnt growing up in a world like this.

I've spread this knowledge among many young individuals and they all agreed with me, that its time we see a change.

Many wise elders that have been my mentor, they all said the same thing that the world needs more people like me. The world needs more world changers.

And after hearing my ideas and vision, after seeing the picture I have painted in their minds of the reality we live in. They have said I am definitely destined to change the world the fact I see the world in this manner at this young age they are more delighted to leave the world in the hands of a motivated, determined and unstoppable young man, like myself.

I couldn't be happier and at peace to hear those words. To know that I am doing something right and I'm walking the right path.

To know that there are people out there who support my crazy idealistic vision that I see for the world.

I couldn't be surer of my goals and dreams. I felt like I've already achieved my success in being the person I was always meant to be.

Even when I was growing up I never liked the way things were, while everyone was too busy following "something" I was questioning everything. Every aspect of life. I think the main reason for this was because I've felt pain too young, felt abandoned and alone. Felt like everything was down to me, because I'm alone and I don't have anyone I have to do everything myself.

So this forced me to think crazy instead what I should have been doing is enjoying my childhood like the other kids like my friends.

I've always separated myself from the crowd always been the one different from the average. All this rage and anger in me, all this pain made me a revolutionist from young.

I soon begun to realise that my parents had no choice to leave me behind they didn't have enough money and because of circumstances in my country, the way society is that's why they had to leave me.

And that's where my disgust for this world begun. That's where I became the crazy idealistic that's coming for the world and everything in it!

'DON'T give your heart to this world, for only pain & self destruction awaits.'

Torture

Torture, torture, torture me a heaven,

Torture, torture, torture My breathing

Torture, torture, torture Me living,

Torture, torture, torture Me a weapon,

Life show me another way

Show me another path to take,

All these spacey thoughts

Make me feel betrayed,

Should I call her

Or shall I tell her to go away,

Here tie me down

And burn my frown,

For I am no longer bound to this earth

Drum on my drums

Till I hear no sound,

Take out my ligament

So I end up like an object,

Get a tissue

And take out my tissues,

Wipe away my tears

And let my heart refuse you,

My skin smooth and soft

Like paper,

Go ahead sketch your art

So I have a story

To tell later,

I think my pain receptors

Stopped working

All I feel is

Tickling,

I can't help but laugh

Till my brain stops

Listening,

All my life's memories

Starts glistening,

One last shine

To make me miss everything,

Cut my skull

Let the juice pour out

Looking menacing,

And Sprinkle the last remains

Of my dreams

As the finishing.

Torture, torture, torture me a heaven,

Torture, torture, torture My breathing

Torture, torture, torture Me living,

Torture, torture, torture Me a weapon,

Torture me

Sometimes I wonder will my life ever change or would it be the way I want it to be like. Why do I love talking about success and self-development? I know the things I've been through have lead me to this very moment of my life. If I had the chance to go back and change anything, I wouldn't change anything. In fact if I had a chance to say one thing to my younger self, I would say learn everything you are going through, keep going and don't let anyone stop you. The world is yours! You are going to love what's about to happen to you in a few years. When I was growing up I was surviving on miseries and always felt like something was trying to tear me apart. I was being tested so much It got to a point where all I could see, is myself in hell being shown an illusion of heaven, but at the same time my skin being pulled off my body and brain melting from the heat of the fire.

A torture that was going to change everything, a happy little child now became a child that became detached from worldly desires. A mind that was now drowned by darkness the only light that remains is the good in him. Death was something he was now ready to embrace but until then he is ready to live and breathe every air he can get. It was this torture that his mind was fighting constantly. It was this torture that would make a better human. It was this torture that would put him ahead of his time. It was this torture that would make him wise. It was this torture that would make him decide to change the world. At this moment he realised that there is no one here but him, no one here to help him and it is always going to be like that. So he decided that he will not let anyone define who he is, he is not going to let anyone stop him, he is coming for the world because the world has hurt him and made him this way. He is not expecting to live through his success, whether he becomes successful or not he knows he will be gone before this happens. So that is why he decided to create something that is going to be here long after he is gone. He is going to touch people's heart, emotions and feelings because that's something you can never get rid of. As long as people have these elements in them even after he is gone he knows he is done well to help people like he always wanted to.

It was from then I started seeing things differently I mean everything was different. I was looking at the world from another dimension. I could see now all the little things the world is hiding and all the little things the world has, that you can have for yourself. I can see how infinite the world is, unlimited treasures all ready for you to take it but people limit themselves thinking it is impossible to do the possible. You are one creation that is free, no restrictions to go wherever you want, do whatever you want and achieve whatever you want. But yet they choose to live with limits and under the illusion that the world shows you of impossibilities.

The world tests you and only if you pass the world will take off its mask and show you what it really is. You'll realise you have been living in a room all this time. A torture like what I went through is one of the many tests the world will throw at you. If you haven't yet been able to see things differently it is because you haven't passed yet. So make sure you pass, let the torture happen to you it is the best thing that will happen to you.

Is it a crime to do what I love, Is it a crime to live a life of being free and happiness. Is it a crime for a broken man dreams to become reality.

Oh god take me away from all this pressure and pain, let my mind explore the knowledge you gave me and let my soul find your love. Don't let me loose myself in this cruel world because life is killing and the people don't care.

All those nights I stayed up and told you that I don't want anything from this world. I know you made me go through all this and you took everything away from me because I know you are going to give me ten times more in return.

You might give it to me in this world or after I die but either way I can't wait to see you. I'm ready and I no longer worry for this place. Until my time comes I will do my part and wait patiently. A lot of people have hurt me but don't punish them as I have forgiven them. Just let me become someone that can help people.

What's your Mirror?

Going back to when I said I begun to think differently, I became even better as a human. Let me give you an example to show you how I saw things differently.

This is how you think and be different.
 If you have two mirrors, one is broken into pieces and one is perfectly fine no scratch nothing which one would you choose and why?

I would choose the broken mirror, because the mirror that's perfect it is always going to be like that it will never change. The shape, the look, it will stay the same and eventually become old. That mirror will have many regrets because it won't be happy with the time it spent. It spent all it's time trying to be perfect and look perfect and didn't want to try anything else. How boring and sad is that! The perfect mirror soon realises that it is not perfect because it is not happy, and there is no such thing as perfection.

Now the broken mirror has many broken pieces, that means you can place the pieces wherever you want and you will still be able to make a mirror. You can make all types of shape; it does not have to look good as long as it does what it is purposed to do. If something doesn't fit right? No big deal you can learn from that mistake and try something else. Try a different piece. You can change it as many times as you like and you are free to go wherever you want. You don't have to be in one place all day long on display, like how the perfect mirror is. You don't have to do the same thing every day because you are broken and you are not perfect, you can choose how you can build yourself back up. You can decide how you put your broken pieces in place.

In fact you are more beautiful and more perfect than the perfect mirror because you will learn way more and you can change as many times till you are happy. The perfect mirror has just one chance either have broken pieces or carry on being the untouched perfect mirror.

The perfect mirror was laughing at the broken mirror because it was different, it was a freak and it was weird. But soon the broken mirror showed all its beauty that it created from the brokenness. The perfect mirror tried to do the same thing but was unsuccessful. The perfect mirror had too many fears and was scared of change. It didn't want to take any risks and it didn't want to take the harder options.

The broken mirror knows all the imperfections it has but

still you can see the same world through those pieces just as you would see the world through the perfect mirror. The broken mirror will have no regrets because it has tried many things, even the failures it has gone through it was able to be something different. What's already broken can't be broken again. So therefore the broken mirror has no limits, has no one stopping it, it is unstoppable and it can be anything. The broken mirror is different and there is no shame in being unique.

Be more like the broken mirror and not like the perfect mirror.

Not so lucky

I'm different from the average because I don't come from a privileged background, but from Background I had to struggle all through my childhood and I had to do everything myself. Now success is just fresh air for me there's way more to it that I have figured out!!

In a way I'm thankful for everything I had to go through because they have made me the person I am. Having no parents around made me feel really down all the time, I had a lot of rage and brokenness inside me.

At a young age I had to carry a lot on my shoulders searching for that one emotion that will bring peace in my heart.

I was always looking for something that filled my emptiness but I never knew what the reason was for me feeling this way. For me to be this way and for me to behave this way.

It brought out this attitude, this other side to me that I had to meet and get to know.

I know it sounds weird but it was like I was a whole different person someone I didn't like. I wanted to do everything I can to change.

All the rage I carried around made me want to achieve more and do better for myself. To prove everyone wrong and mostly to prove myself wrong, that I'm not some useless, hopeless, abandoned little kid.

All these thoughts in my head, eating away at my brain cells, causing me great discomfort. Started seeing life in different perspectives, started thinking about how death would feel like, started wishing that I don't wake up Tomorrow, started praying to my creator to take me to him I wanted to be with him nothing else.

But it seemed like the more I wanted to be with him the more he kept me away, kept me alive to test me, how much I really love my creator how much I really love the life he gave me.

So I begun to appreciate everything humbled myself and realised that all these materialistic objects like money wasn't important. All the things that I thought was important just became less important worse then just dirt to me. The peace I simply got by accepting all my imperfections by accepting all my emotions and forgiving everyone that has ever hurt me made me unlock many qualities, felt like I just unlocked every single power there was, a whole universe was accessible to just me.

Felt like my body was still attached to this world but my soul was flying exploring the world felt unstoppable.

All this happened by me lowering my pride, realising that I

am nothing but a body made from flesh and blood. I knew that I didn't have to carry the world's worries; I didn't have to save the ones that didn't want to be saved. I don't have to free the world from these invisible chains that can really mess someone up.

I remember when that one person you really love and all the memories, all the things they promised you will soon be destroyed by a heart break that will ruin everything within you. You are stuck in one place trapped by a movie on constant replay killing you slowly like a snake biting you every time you try to forget.

I was unable to do anything, I stopped why I'm not happy, I know I'm not Rich or famous but even with all the small blessings in my life why am I not happy?

Why do we as humans always want more? Why can't we be happy with what we already have? We don't notice all the blessings we already have in our life, that some of us are able to eat three times a day, eating a warm meal around a table with our families, being able to sleep in our warm comfy beds and wear nice clothes whenever we feel like it. But still it's not enough?

I was broken for so long I still think I am. It hurts so bad no matter what I do its always there I can't get rid of it. Some nights after being so strong I couldn't help it but breakdown because what I had was real and I gave my love to someone that didn't appreciate it.

I was always missing love from my life especially when I was growing up and as a kid you need love every child needs love otherwise it will mess with your head and rewire your brain.

I was looking for something to find that love and the one time I got it, it all ended and shattered me into pieces and took me back to the broken abandoned little boy.

I was scared that the love I have for her does not turn into hate and sometimes I feel like if I ever saw her I would want to shoot her for all the times she made my heart suffer.

But I knew that was just my anger speaking.

It just felt like I was looking for her in other people all the time, I was looking for her love in everything I do and it felt like no matter how hard I try I can't let her go and move on. But I did move on because I started focusing on me more and less on others.

I believe that the way society is structured makes it harder for people like me to succeed. The less advantaged have to work twice as harder just to prove something. Let's face it, if we look at history the ones that most benefited were rich, higher class or white. This is something we can't deny because it is history. A lot of people today have forgotten their history or they are not learning about it any more. There is still people killing each other, there Is still high knife crime, high gun crime, high murder rates, there is still racism and yes there is still forms of slavery. If you disagree, I would love to see some proof to show me that these things are not happening. Because believe me I can show you a lot of dark stuff that will get you questioning where you have been living all this time. Or even better go on YouTube and watch some videos of how some kids are living in less developed countries or how some women are being kept as slaves.

I didn't want to put this bit in my book but I guess every

experience I went through made me who I am today so I just kept this in here.

'At first they say they love you & then act like they don't know you'.

Missing you.

I've been missing you,

But your gone away,

I've been missing you,

It's killing me everyday,

I've been missing you,

Tell me what you going through,

Did you even love me tell me it was true,

She was the one that I liked,

Empty brown eyes,

But she couldn't be mine,

Because of all the emotions she kept up inside,

If I didn't have her it would be suicide,

Darkness surrounds me because she was my light,

Trapped in this place I'm loosing my sight,

Dreaming about her every single night,

Please tell me How this is not a sign?

It's clear that it's her that I miss,

It got to a point,

I picked up a pen & wrote this,

Heart aches & rage that's all there is,

Because I made a mistake making her my happiness,

It was all lies she didn't mean it,

She said she will always be there,

But when I needed her most she wasn't there,

After everything we talked about guess you didn't care,

U said you are too damaged so you can't,

It didn't matter to me,

Because you are the only one that I want,

You ruined my sleep you ruined my nights,

Now everything I do I can't get it right,

You know it's funny how you are scared of heights,

Giving me hopes & taking me high,

Remember every time I looked at you I just had to smile,

Because your pretty face made it all worth while,

Just wanted you,

I didn't want anything,

Couldn't careless about the world

But now I want everything,

Because I needed something to fill in the space,

That you left behind,

I want it all because I don't feel fulfil without seeing your face,

I do not like talking about this, but I guess I have to because it shows the old me. All of this and everything I went through made me so much stronger, wiser and unstoppable.

I begun to be less nice to people, begun to be more selfish simple because I didn't want to get hurt again.

I had begun to hate everyone because no one helped me NO ONE!! I always had to fight all this on my own.

This is why I wanted to become someone so great so bad because when I do then I want all these fake people that pretended they are my friend and they care, want to show them what now! You probably thought I'm a nobody, a dumb so called looser huh. What now! Don't come to me all the fake nonsense.

I was giving something to world; I was always giving so much to the world but was getting nothing back.

The one thing I didn't realise that while I was trying to save the world and be a hero, the world was actually making me into a villain.

I don't know what I'll be in the future; I wouldn't be surprised if I became the villain. I'll probably either save the world or destroy it like it destroyed me.

My heart is so cold, dark and in rage. I'm so angry always angry with myself with the world with the people of the world. Angry with all the people who hurt me took everything away from me.

I'm trying to help the world change the world help people

because it helps me heal my heart. Now if that don't work out? Or if that is taken away from me, then I have no option but to see myself become hell itself.

I'm been through enough failure and I'm ready to go through more I won't give up but everyone has their limits and one day I will eventually give up and give in to the darkness the pain that haunts me.

The weaker you are the stronger you are and you will be. My motivation levels are off the rector scale, it's crazy. Right now I'm at the lowest point of my life and there is no going any more lower. I've been here so many times its home for me. I live here. At first I hated it, but now I love it because it pushes me so far over the mountain and over the beyond.

There was times where I used to wear the same clothes for weeks, starve so many nights. I go to sleep starving because I didn't have any change to buy a meal. Living alone in a room made me feel like I was in prison the same 4 white plain walls I see every time and the same plain white ceiling I stare at every night.

I've been hungry for too long, and I'm still hungry more than ever. I want it more than ever.

I don't ever want to come out the low point; I don't ever want to have a full stomach, I don't ever want to feel loved. I want all the pain the struggle there is because I love it and because if I don't have those things then I'll forget about helping people, I'll forget where I came from, I'll forget about the no good for nothing failure I am, I'll forget about all the people I have to prove wrong, I'll forget about being the most amazing little kid that grew up to do extraordinary things.

I want to see the faces of all the beings that made feel worthless and made me feel like I was nothing but dirt, a helpless little waste of space.

Why are you surprised? I told you I am a big deal so deal with me. Deal with it or move out my way because I'm bringing the big storm that I've been fighting all this time. Don't worry, if you think you won't be able to make it through the storm I'm here I'll show you how to do.

"I believe our children are the future, teach them well and let them lead the way" – Whitney Houston

Escape the negative realm.

Why me, why always me. Why am I so depressed? Why am I not happy with my life right now? Why does it have to be this way? These are some of the thoughts that you might have time to time right? Believe me I used to always think like that, it got me questioning everything. It was so easy for me to end up in the negative world. We need to realise that this is how we end up with depression and all of the other things that will ruin you. I always say to people, 'know your WHYS not your WANTS'. Stop thinking about all things you want and how nice it will be to have them. Start thinking about why do you want them? Is it something you really need? Will it make you happy? Why do you want to start a business? Why do I want to buy a car? Why do I want to fall in love? Why do I want to be able to do what I love? Why do I want to travel the world? Now take a look at how I started this paragraph, with all the negative whys. Now look at how I changed that to whys that actually make you think positive. I might be able to guess the answers to these whys you have in your head right now. Most of your answers will relate to some form of you feeling good. The reason for those answers might be a connection to an emotion to make you feel happy and content.

This is all just a mind-set game; it depends on how you are thinking and how the layout of your mind-set is like. Some people cannot help it when something bad happens to them they straight away the first thing that comes in their head is negative thinking. It's like they are almost wired to function that way. But I good news for you, you can rewire your brain. So that next time you will know exactly how to escape the negative realm.

People that always complain, that are not patient or appreciative of where they are in life they will never be happy no matter what position they may be. Whether they are rich or poor they will never be happy because they will always find something to complain about or will not be grateful for the blessings that they have been given. You'll realise soon as we get put in a bad situation the first thing that we think about the bad things that going to happen. We think about all the things that could go wrong for us. Straight away the nerves, anxiety, panic, and stress and worries kick in. we give ourselves up to the negative thoughts, to the negative side to our brain and now we are unable to think straight or make good decisions. Because of the negativity that is clouding our brain we are unable to think clearly.

When you see pain you see negative energy when I see pain I see success.

If your living your life day by day as it comes then I'll tell you right now you are wasting time just pack it in and go sleep! You can't live life just as it comes along hoping for something to happen because I'll tell you nothing will happen! You need to plan and set goals! Set aims and objectives! Have a target you want to hit!

The only way you can really escape the negative realm is if you learn and practice being positive every day. By this I don't mean just the thinking but the actions as well. First comes the thinking then you follow that through with the action. If there is no action after the thinking then it will be a waste because the thinking will disappear soon after when you forget. However if there is action, you will remember that. Because not only you are thinking about it but now you are applying that physically or practically. If you do this most of the days of the week or even everyday, it will become a routine.

Most people find the thinking bit the hardest but it's not that hard once you figure out how your mind works and once you know yourself well enough. You have to learn how to unlock your mind; I know it sounds like something an air bender would say from Avatar. But that is exactly what you have to do. Or like in Naruto you have to learn how to control your nine tails chakra to reach greater powers. Sorry about these references I am an anime geek.

Everyone has different ways of unlocking their inner powers. The human mind is one unstoppable creation; it is the only thing that has no limits to how far it can go. Your eyes can not see that far only to certain limit, your ears won't be able to hear that far, your arms won't be able to reach that far but your mind no limit at all.

Go far and over the beyond to the unknown, let the mind travel on its promised journey. Unlock the perfect dimension. Create new ideas and innovations for the future. Discover the positive energy that overpowers the dark.

Sleep paralysis!

It was that day when I was

Asleep on my bed,

Eyes half open don't know if I'm dead,

Blurred vision & hearing voices in my head,

Was it a dream or was it reality instead,

Body paralysed from the awakening of pain, the silent tears from my past drowning my brain,

Trying to move but my body won't listen,

Rejecting any instructions I give it,

Maybe it's sleep paralysis or maybe it is not, deciding to fight or to just give in,

Is it a wakeup call I've been missing?

The trembling fear that has risen,

The regret of me not loving,

The regret of me not living,

Has my time come is this death?

Am I proud the way my life was lead,

I know I'm a failure I know I'm a mess,

No one will even know about my sadness,

Why do I sound depressed all the time,

Are these thoughts even mine?

When I'm around people I always smile,

Maybe I'm just out of my mind,

I'm trying to lift my fingers,

Lift my hand up,

Feels like my soul is flying,

But my body won't wake up,

Finally the sleep paralysis leaves me alone,

After fighting me all on its own,

Disappearing, it's completely gone,

But I know it will come back to claim its throne.

Patience

 I'm always taking my time I've always had patience there was times where I just said to myself I need to be successful now! This can't wait, and there was times where I was just like what's the rush let time catch up to me and let life write the rest of my story just let it play out. Patience is the key! Anyway I still need to see who else will betray me who else will have no hope in me, who else won't believe in me and I need to see who else I'm going to prove wrong. It is fun trust me. I like the challenge I like the doubts, makes it even more worth it in the end. All this time I've stayed silent watching the world and its people carefully, you can say I've been taking notes. The world is going through a phase right now where you will see all the people that act a bit crazy and doing crazy things are becoming famous and rich while the intellectual individuals are labelled as boring and not fun. But there is going to come a time when the roles will be reversed and the intellectual people will begin to rule the world begin to change the world. Me? I'm just waiting for my time to come I know now it's too soon for me to come my time is way later. Even if I had the chance now I would not take it, it's too soon.

If your living your life day by day as it comes then I'll tell you right now you are wasting your time just pack it in and go sleep! U can't live life just as it comes along, hoping for something to happen because I'll tell you nothing will happen! You need to plan and set goals! Set aims & objectives! Have a target you want to hit! Work your hardest for the next five years of your life.

Don't worry about what people are doing or what people are saying. Even if someone else is doing better than you or it might seem that way. Don't ever compare yourself to someone else. Everyone has their own path to walk so the road they are taking is way different than you.

Be happy for others. When you see others succeed don't feel jealous but feel happy and say it is their time and they did well. Say soon it will be my time just like them; it's not here because I'm not ready and I need to work harder and keep going.

I know everything you have been through or currently going through it is not easy. Some of those things might be hurting you, causing you to not see the good that awaits you. Unfortunately there is nothing you can do about that pain. There is no way of stopping it. But what you can do is not let that take any control of the future you.

"There are two kinds of companies, those that work to try to charge more and those that work to charge less. We will be the second." – Jeff Bezos

Broken

What I don't understand is that how can people even have the heart to hurt others. Like let's say there is someone you really love and you were about to build an amazing future together. You get so attached that you can't imagine living your life with anyone but that person. A big part of that is that they made you feel a special way that you have never felt before. A sense of happiness that is so powerful that you have forgotten every ounce of pain you have ever felt. A person that has that kind of effect on you, now how can you not want to be with someone like that?

I was broken for so long because that person didn't want to be with me after we both thought that we will be together forever. She blocked me, she stopped answering my calls and she stopped texting. Within moments it was like we never really knew each other at all. Within moments nothing meant anything and it was all gone.

I reached out but I was reaching out to emptiness. All of a sudden it was all quiet and I had to return to the dark, unwanted room I was in before.

So many times I sat there thinking why did this happen to me. Why would god give me something like that only to remove it from my life?

Maybe it was to teach me something, maybe it was a lesson I had to learn. Maybe god changed his mind or maybe he didn't. Or maybe it was something to make me stronger and give me a reason to become a success.

Maybe I'm just cursed and I will never have that. Maybe it just is not for me. And maybe I'll be long gone before I can have that.

But whatever it may be, I'll focus on me becoming successful. If it is for me then when the time is right it will come to me. For now I need to achieve my goals and be happy with the process I'm currently in.

To all who have been broken in the past don't let it get you down, trust me life changes and it becomes better. I can finally say that looking back at how I was before, to how I've changed and become a better me.

I've used all of that as motivation to make something of

myself, to become something great. And you should too. Keep going it gets better trust me!

Money Sickness

Last night I had a dream,

Money pouring in,

I was going to be rich,

More than anything,

It was money that I wanted

And happiness that I needed,

The two combined

Was the perfect fantasy?

I'm waiting for the day

They tell me they believed in me,

Yeah right you didn't even listen to me,

I made 7 Mill & that was no joke

I made 20 Mill & that was no joke,

I make money when I rise &

Even I fall,

So I make money regardless if I blow,

Never tell them how much paper you own,

Nowadays you have to just act like you are broke,

They get jealous when you make it on your own,

That's a path to success man

Come tell me if you know,

I got that real shine I got that good life glow,

Success after success I'm on roll,

Money after money all in row,

I got that crazy, I'll get mine flow,

What's a good day & what's bad luck,

What's money & power if your broke & stuck,

You never been there,

You never been that,

You never had to struggle,

You never seen that,

Money got me feeling high,

Money got me feeling low,

Money in my head,

All anyone knows,

Money is everything,

Money is pride,

Money is life,

But you can't take it when you die,

Money to the ceiling,

Damn it's like that?

Triple that investment,

& pull it right back,

I'm a hustler man

You should have known that,

I had all the facts & numbers

Right from the start,

You was part my plan,

You was part of my game,

The pawn that helped me on the right lane,

When I think about it man

That was quite evil,

That's what happens

When you mess with my sequel,

This is my story,

This is my film,

You can't match me,

I'm in a different realm,

Bank or not,

Money won't stop,

Money is my crop,

Make money till I drop,

Poor heart rich mind,

This that money sickness

That's a sad life to live,

But somehow you still feel priceless,

So now you got to know your worth,

Is it money that you want,

Or you want to stunt,

Either way you will have to work,

Either way you will have to run.

"Success is a lousy teacher. It seduces smart people into thinking they can't lose." – Bill Gates

For lot of the time I always used to hear successful people say be what you love and do what you love, then find a way to make a living from that. Heck, I was even saying it to a lot of people to do that. That you should follow your passion which is right I'm not saying there is anything wrong with that. I was saying that if there is not a job out there that you love? Well then create a job that you love!

The reason why I am talking to you about this is because a lot of the time I forgot to ask the very same question and wisdom to myself. I forgot to ask myself what I loved doing and what do I want to be doing for a living.

Confusion hit me so hard, that I almost started following what people were doing out there and forcing myself to think that I also liked doing that. But I didn't. I soon figured out what I loved doing but I had one issue with that, I didn't know how I was going to make money from it. How was I going to make a living? The funny thing is I never cared about the money part till people started asking me "yes but how are going to make money from that Mitak?" that's the type of sentence I had to hear all the time. It frustrated me, annoyed me and definitely made me go crazy with rage because everyone completely missed what I was trying to say. I would speak so passionately and lovingly about my dreams and goals. All I hear in return is money, money & money.

It was like people became so attached to money that they saw no other purpose to life, if it didn't include money. They was unable to look at the bigger picture and think outside the box for once. People didn't want to hear or understand the vision any more because all they cared about was money.

Even now I have no idea what so ever how I will make money all I know is I want to be doing what I love for the rest of my life regardless. Money became such a powerful and important aspect to people that they are ready to step over someone else to get it. Whether that's doing fraud, scams, crime, you name it! Anything! Just to gain money. Money has ruined humans and I'll say that hands down. It's facts and it's the truth. It has ruined mankind so much that systems and certain types of societies were created. Your even classed as something in the living world. Working class, middle class and higher class. Just think about it, why do you think they don't teach you about money in school? Because your job is not to learn how to manage money, your job is to be a good little worker and stay in line. How comes you don't know how to invest your money? How comes you don't understand what true financial freedom is? How comes you don't know about assets? The rich know and so does the higher class people, that's not fair. That's not being equal is it?

Well I'll let you think about that for a while. Coming back to what I was saying... I don't know how money will play into my goals and dreams. But what I do know is that it will make me someone really powerful, respected and successful. All I know is that I love motivating others, helping others, bringing change, innovations, ideas, creativity, teaching others, sharing wisdom, giving advice, being an activist on improving the world, writing, speaking in front of millions of people which I will do eventually and so much more. Money has been the last thing I thought about. The only time I had to sit there and think money makes the world go around? Is when I get pushed to the edge, starving and restless to survive. Money slowed me down so much. Because I needed to eat and live, that automatically became my first priority which I disliked. It pushed me away from why I was here, pushed me away from my goals and ambitions. However I didn't let that stop me once, I had that clear one goal in mind and that's to achieve my ultimate dreams for the future.

We need to stop being so serious and realistic all the time. For once everyone needs to let their creativity and imagination run marathons across the galaxy. Have you heard that saying "anything is possible" well if that's the case then stop limiting yourself with too much realism. Like when was the last time you thought but robots doing jobs or an AI tech that can solve problems on its own?

Here is the good news that time is closer than you think because someone out there didn't let anything stop them from going wild with their ideas. Imagine your grandma in her times saying, what if we had a device that let me talk to other people without me actually being there? Or what if this telephone was wireless and didn't have all these uncomfortable buttons and I could give it voice commands, even ask it something like what's the weather like tomorrow? Imagine Steve Jobs or Disney never asked a what if question to themselves and instead they just said "oh that's silly, come on how can we even create something like that?". Well I think you get the point here. So let me ask you this, we're all these extraordinary minds thinking about how can I make money?

I always believed that just go out there and do what makes you feel complete, you are here for a reason so go and fulfil that reason. Stop worrying about materialistic objects or digital fame and appreciation. Start thinking about what can I do to make this a better place? What is the part I have to play here? Why do I want to do the things I want to do?

When you just put yourself out there and start doing what you love? Everything else will just follow as if almost they are incomplete without you.

Look at it this way, you can waste your time trying chase a dragon fly, but if you have what the dragon fly wants it will come to you. I mean dragon flies are very rare nowadays especially here in the UK. You probably will see one or two if you are lucky in the summer time when it's really hot. But just how rare a dragon fly is, likewise achieving success is also very rare. Therefore if you want success figure what that means to you, is it being rich or is it being in a place of mind you want to be.

I did that

Look at my life,
Look at what I been through,
I been there & done that,
Made it out & ate it up like a snack,

Fake people showing fake love,
All I ever did was show you real love,
But I'll look past that,
Because people like that will always be last,

Raised myself? I did that,
Self taught? I did that,
Self made? I did that,
Suicide me? H I tried that,
But I'm still here huh,

No ones listening so I'm still working,
I speak my mind because a lot of things is not working,
Drowning in darkness
still feel like I'm missing something,
Was it desire or was it wanting,

I didn't want much I didn't want all that,
I guess the best revenge is,
When you live the life

They want,

Now I'm wondering if I should let bygones be bygones,
Because a lot of people hurt me
I did nothing wrong,
Now I'm the bad guy,
Now I'm the bad son,

Okay then...

Time

Time is not promised to no man or woman. We keep saying that we're not ready right now we will be ready later on, how do you know that later on is Guaranteed? ' I'll wait till I'm financially stable then I'll get married' or 'let me make this much amount of money then I can start my business' or ' let me have few more cigarettes then I'll stop' or 'I'm still young I'll start my diet later' but having said all of that, it does not mean you rush into things either.

Time is a process and a moment that you get only once. After that time has gone that moment has gone you are not able to bring it back. Time is really fragile, soft and special you have to look after it and always be cautious of how you are making the most of it.

Energy compliments time, you ask how? Well depending on the energy you are providing, time returns that favour back to you with results. So if you have positive energy and you are using your time wisely with that energy, really making a difference then just imagine the results that you will create. A positive result right? Of course! That's how it works!

Well you know that saying 'what you put in is what you get out' to a certain extent that is true depends on your perspective and how you look at things.

Time also plays a big part when you are in pain, suffering,

struggling or going through hard times in your life. When things are not going well. A lot of people forget that the hardships that we go through are only temporary and that it will pass soon. I used to see it as something that stops me in my tracks and hated it. But now I've realised that what we go through makes us who we are, makes us stronger and makes us wiser. It's a lesson we learn. And for me? It's like therapy to get back up and shine even brighter; it's an upgrade for me every time. Now when I go through hardships I know it's only time testing me and developing me to be even better and I know when I come out of this I'm going to be on another level.

So we need to know that it's only temporary, it's only time doing its part and you are not going to be in that situation forever it will be over now it's all down to you. Be patient, smart, positive, caring, kind and focus on the future how to better yourself and teach yourself to deal with it. It won't go away I'll tell you that now pain, suffering and struggle is always going to be just in different forms but what makes it easy is how you learn to deal with it. Once you know how to handle it and deal with it, it will make it so much easier for you till you won't even know it's there any more. But to get to that level you need to appreciate and be patient when you are in those situations. And look at the situation you are in and look at the energy you are providing!

Taking risks & on the grind

In the morning he shall devour the prey,
& in the evening he shall divide the spoils. If you don't devour when you are young? You'll have nothing to divide when your old. - T.D Jakes

This really hit me, made me understand the true nature of the grind. What does it mean to really work for what I want? How do I know if I'm on the grind? I started thinking and looking back at every step I took. Everything I've done until this moment. What did I do? How did I spend my time? At first I was worried because what if the answer will be you didn't do enough. But I was wrong, I did do enough.

I worked so hard, gave it my all.

Everyday I would work on my dreams, wake up early in the morning or go sleep late at night. Reading books, watching videos, following successful people and even attending networking events to connect with people from all walks of life. Strangely enough, Somehow I feel like I didn't do enough, like I could have done way more. Really pushed myself to the limits and give it my all. Till I run out of breath or till I collapse into nothingness. Till my eyes became watery, red and sore. Till I could no longer stand up because of the fatigue. Until all the muscles in my body could no longer move, except for the muscle that puts a smile on my face. A huge smile from all the excitement and dopamine I get from grinding. That's how I wanted to work, like there is no tomorrow. Like I was short on time.

That's exactly how I started to work and I soon begun to see the results right in front of my eyes. It was amazing! It's still is!

I rather work and suffer now then work and suffer when I'm old. When I have no more energy left and I'm no longer in my prime. That's when I should be relaxing and enjoy the remaining humble days.

I always felt like I'm constantly on the run, I had this weird uneasy feeling all the time. This feeling made me feel restless like I always needed to do something. Like I wasn't safe and secure. I was constantly fighting for my survival, I still am now. I can't stop, it's too soon. And at that point, for the first time in my life, I knew that this is what it means to live life in your own terms. To live a life full of risks and adventure, to be in control and most importantly to be free. At this point I knew that this is what it means to really grind. To really build something, from real blood, sweat and tears. To understand the meaning behind how powerful you can be when you put yourself to work. Want to know the best part to all this? Is that you really just proved to yourself that you can do something that you thought you never could do. You built something with your bare hands from nothing.

The days I was jobless and couldn't get a job was the biggest risk I took. The day I quit my part time job and said no this is not it for me there is more to why I am here. I took the biggest risk. I put myself in a position where I had no choice, I had to grind and push myself. It was only then I unlocked my true potentials and understood the real reason why I was here.

I had no income, no money coming in to help me survive. That was a test in itself, to really see what I'm made of. A lot of people want that 9-5 job because it's a sense of security but the bad thing about that? Is that you will never know who you truly are. What talents you have hidden inside you. All you will be doing is following someone's step by step to do a job. Make someone else rich and ruin your self worth. I stepped out of my comfort zone and decided to stop living comfortably. There is a reason why I want more, why I have all these dreams, so that means I have to go get what's mine.

If I said to you, whatever you speak into existence, have a sense of belief that is so strong and have faith, it will come true. Would you believe me? I used to think that was nonsense, until I started doing exactly that. But that being said does not mean you just believe and it will happen, you still have to play your part and put some actions into play. Just like a game if I created the most powerful player, it would not make me the most powerful player until I actually played the game and win.

When you put words into action, you will see that it becomes true. I speak it everyday, "I am going to be so successful." "I will be everything they said I cannot" "what I'm going through right now will make me someone amazing." "I am going to be so rich." "I am going to help so many people." "I will change so many people's lives."

The work ethic has to be so extreme that no matter how many times you fail, it will only bring you closer to your goal. Most people give up after few failed attempts and they say that this is not for me, it's not working out. The reason why you failed, the reason why it is not for you, is because that is the thing that will take you to what is meant for you. Its a process not the destination. This is the process that will get you to your destination. Now if you don't put in the work how do you expect to reach the destination? Bring you dreams and goals into fruition. Live it, and work for it, no matter what storm or rain befalls you.

Where I am right now in my life- 2018

Right now everything is going better then what it used to be like. I've become better I've grown up more. I've become more clearer on my goals and what I want to do. I found some things that I really love doing. One of those things is reading every single day, I never stop learning. Now I'm always looking for places where I can gain knowledge. I stopped going out and stay in mostly doing work. I have realised that I have to make some sacrifices now in order to enjoy those things later. It's all going to be worth it later on right? I have decided to use the year 2018 to just build myself up and start working on a foundation.

It is august now and I've been planning to launch my business by end of 2019. I've been working with Prince's trust to help build a successful business and I have also been working with my mentors on this exciting new journey. Meeting up with my mentors every few months helps a lot, they give me brilliant advice as well support me with my business plan. I won't go into what my business is etc. Maybe you want to do a research on that to find that out. But I'll leave it for now.

I started with the question of why would people want to buy my business? But I soon realised that this question was only going to bring me down.

When I started my business I always had that one question that kept giving me second thoughts and kept holding me back. Why would anyone want to invest their time and money into my business? What makes my business different and unique that customers or clients would want to buy from? Those questions made it so much harder for me even though my motivation levels were really high.

The question that I should ask myself is, why do I even

want to do this? After I asked this question, everything became clear. I knew my reason and I know my why and what I must do.

The way my mind-set was at that time was that I always thought about what could go wrong for me. I thought about my own self destruction before anyone else did. Now that is not always a bad thing, it's good to think about those thoughts as it prepares you for the worse, plus you get to plan ahead and prevent it from ever happening. However having said that what is bad is the over thinking, panicking and the negative energy you feed it. Once you do that you have lost.

I always say there is always two ways to dealing with a problem or a situation. You can deal with it by having a positive perspective towards it or deal with it from a negative perspective, your choice.

From that moment I began to look at life and its problems in a different perspective. I began to face all my fears that I had waiting inside me.

I'm going to be big one day, and I know it. This is my

destiny, that's how I saw it. Give happiness to my pain because I owe it. Never will I fall because I've already been through it.

If you are already on the grind, already hustling then you are winning. However if you are not then you are losing big time. You don't need flashy lights and cameras for you to know you are successful. You don't need seven digits in your bank account to tell you are successful. All you need is happiness and contentment within yourself. Then you will see that all of that will come after automatically, it will all come chasing you.

Let's be real.

There were so many days I would not want to do anything. My anxiety would take over my body. I start feeling like vomiting for no reason. When I was little I use to just sit somewhere before I came home from school or when I was out and just sit and think how things would be different if I had my mum and dad with me. How people won't treat me differently. I think about those who are less unfortunate than me. I think about those who have holes in their clothes and ripped up shoes. They steal a piece of bread just to survive and eat. The shop keeper instead of helping the poor child he will give one back hand slap across the face. Yes this still happens it's not just in movies in fact where do you think they got these ideas from to actually put it in a movie?

Thinking about those things actually made me feels worse because I wanted to just get up and help them. But I was the one in need of help.

I used to like sitting there alone I guess it was the only time I could be in a peace of mind and just reflect on my life. I knew if I went to home wherever that is, I would not be able to be myself and have some real time like that.

I thought about what my mum would be doing at this time and what about my little sister how is she like now? What does she like? What's her favourite colour? If she was here I could have played with her and watch her grow up. Is she happy and does she have the chance to be a child and live her childhood properly? Unlike me I didn't get the chance to be a kid I was too busy thinking about why I feel pain and why my life is like this and why are people treating me like this?

I watched other kids with their parents going home from school felt really happy for them that they have something like that but I felt jealous and sad at the same time. So I carried on sitting there and that thought cycled back about how my life will be like if I had my parents.

My stomach started making noises I guess I was hungry. But I felt guilty even eating. I was living someone else's house that I always to think I'm staying in their house and I'm eating their food. I never felt like I ever owned anything of mine.

Yes this woman and this family were raising me, but I always felt like I didn't belong there. I knew I didn't belong. Maybe she was just keeping me for the money who knew. I didn't really feel like eating I don't know I was very suicidal maybe I'll just die from hunger and all this will be over. I can finally see my creator and ask him what the reason for my life being that way was.

I thought about the future if this is it for me, this is how the rest of my life will be like. No one came to my rescue and no one helped me.

I might not even get a job because my grades will be so low. I'm so messed up right now I can't even remember anything. I was shaking especially my hands and I began to see bright white lights in my left eye. The right side of head was hurting so mad like a big needle was going through me skull.

It was an anxiety attack and a migraine.

I couldn't breathe for few seconds, started huffing and puffing for air. I started crying I don't know why but everything that was hurting me came out. But the tears were so slow and warm. It was as if it was taking it's time to make sure it gets rid of all the pain.

There was a lot going through my mind, I felt like there were always times like this but it just wasn't as bad as when I used to sit there alone.

These moments were the reason why I wanted to just end it all because I couldn't bear the pain.

One line I used to always say is that I don't know what I did to deserve this.

Khaos

you want to be free
You want to be seen
Khaos in your mind
Khaos is me,

Trying to escape,
Trying to go far,
you limit yourself,
So that's discard,

So tell em what you want,
Do you want to live or run,
Are you claiming the moon or
are you claiming the sun,
Do you want to breathe or are you done,
Do you want peace or you want a gun,
Have you really lost or have you won?

So tell me what's it going to be,
Is it freedom or slavery that you miss,

Is it the hateful words you want to say,
Or is it living a miserable day,
Take me where it is safe,
Take me to that happy place,

See the world around you and wake up,
Some kids in the world don't even get to wake up, they
will be lucky to even see a plate, while you sit here and
just complain,

my mind is racing in different speeds,
I always speak it real whenever I need,
I don't need no fake love to seal me,
I don't need no poison to kill me,

Destruction & pain,
No I don't want no deal,
I don't want no fame,
The world is in khaos,
Things need to change,

You want to act tough you want to be the man,
One thing I don't understand,

Your still self concerned,
When you got all the opportunities in your hand,

Stay woke and live life,
My mum taught me to never take sides,
Don't take shit from people
Don't live a lie,
Live true and do what's right,

Stand up for your people and fight,
A true revolutionist that cried but still smiled,
that's who I inspire to be like,

So set your mind free,
And break from this destruction,
Where your nothing but a torture
And a slave to this system,

Your heart is in love with this illusion,
You need to win no matter what because that's your
conclusion,

A gruesome war and havoc that you are not seeing,
Because you are made to believe that this place your in?
Is called living,

you want to be free

You want to be seen
Khaos in your mind
Khaos is me.

What is peace when your mind is burning, screaming, raging with anger and all these bright colours ripped apart from this sickening oil, dissolving my organs till murder feeds me. Freedom is the biggest thief and trust is nothing but a leaf. My crime is okay as long as I have an excuse. Therefore I want to kill and slaughter whoever may be amused. I'll tell the brothers and my gang get your sticks and forks, start digging. For all the betrayal, for all the emotions, broken hearts, broken relationships, get me her hair so I can burn it all down till it becomes blooded ashes and disappears. It's time for revenge, I'm here to collect my repayment and taxes. So put your head in this soil, suffocate yourself till I am satisfied and for interest eat the worms that you once tried to make me eat. Now sit up and let me watch my ants enter through your nose till you get nose bleed. Let me enjoy the view of you fidgeting while I use a hacksaw on your neck joint.

When your broke and people laugh in your face, you just want to engrave your initials on their pupils. I used to think these cyan flames was hot and infamous until I conquered this illusion of fear, and realised it was actually freezing cold. This mirage was made to show how fearsome it could be. But before I knew it, I became numb. Been hustling all my life, sacrifices all my life. Married to the game, a legend in this life, I want to play today and I want to die tomorrow. I designed myself, gave me some colour and game me some nails.

You are my breathing corpse, let me give you some stripes on your skin from your shoulder blade to your finger tips.

Change your thinking.

'I know I'm going to be successful it's only matter of time.'

I was stuck in this place for a really long time. No matter how hard I tried thinking positive thoughts, I was unable to escape this place of negativity. I failed a lot in the past with whatever I did. This was one of the main reasons why I always ended up there. Failures would get to me so bad that I didn't want to get up from bed any more. Just felt like giving up. At times I just couldn't handle everything life put me through, so I thought about being dead and how that will solve everything. But I also knew that it won't. There is a reason why I am here and there is a reason why I am going through all this. I might not know the exact answer to why, but I know that something good is coming for me. Maybe I won't be rich and everything however I know that it will change me for the better and make me a better person. That's for sure. I've changed so much over the years and these struggles have force me to be something amazing. I know I am still young and I have so much more experiences that still have to get a taste for. There is so much more that life still needs to test me on. I'm just getting ready for all of that.

Over the years I've had a lot of people telling me that I won't be able to make it, it's really hard out there. They all pointed out my mistakes and pointed out the amount of times I have failed. But not once did any of them tell me that this is only the start and I will be successful. Everyone wants to talk about how "your ideas might not work", "people might not be interested in what you have to offer" and I like this one "it's a big risk you have to take". These phrases are the most poisonous and downgraded thoughts you could have or even say to someone. It will put others down and make them think they have no hope in achieving their dreams. These sentences are the exact reason why most people either give up or don't have any belief in succeeding. If you have this way of thinking let me tell you change it now! And I mean now! It is dangerous because it will grow on you and become part of your comfort zone. It will be so easy for you to utter these words and hard for you to utter any positivity. Don't let it become part of you just keep it as a recycling brain cell that you will convert into a positive energy. It's fine to have thoughts like this but the more time you spend thinking about these things the more you will be drowning yourself. If you decide to act on these thoughts you have giving it confirmation and have invited it in to live with you forever.

When I started my business it was really frustrating because I was struggling to get clients. No one really believed in my business. I had to constantly make changes and keep updating. It was a learning process for me in fact it still is.

I always knew that it will take time, a process that you can't rush. There was many times where I had thoughts of just giving up; I always thought that this is not going to work. I have too much competition and why would anyone want to buy into my business? These two thoughts started off as a negative cycle that gave me every reason to just pack it in and let go. I don't know but something didn't let me give up, I've been through too many hardships to quit now. I want to be free and do what I love; this is going to be worth it. I know it! That's what I kept telling myself until I begun to actually live by those words. Soon it became a part of who I am and guess what? I just made these thoughts become positive. Now I asked myself what can I do differently from my competition and I must give a reason why people should buy into me not my business. Remember people are not just buying products or services, but they are investing their precious time and money into you. So make them believe in you and make them feel that it is the only right thing to do.

Don't make decisions on emotions and don't make

decisions thinking that it will work out eventually. Make decisions based on how you think about the future you truly want. What do you value most? Is it happiness that you are truly after? Or is it a sense of feeling financially secured?

If you are angry don't make a decision wait till you calm down, and you are able to think straight. Because we will make a mistake and then regret the decision we have made. If you are upset and down don't make a decision based on that. Because likewise you might regret the decision you have made. A decision will come to you as a thought first before you decide to act on it. While it is still a thought that's the best time to explore all the other options, ask yourself what you value most in life. If it is something that make you feel good or something that goes against your value then make the decision in the right way.

You don't want to upset anyone but let them know that you are firm with the decision you have made, and they have to respect that.

Change your thinking. If you are constantly thinking about the negative that is happening in your life, then that's all you are going to get. However if you change the way you think and change the way you look at life, you will notice that you are in control, now decide which one you want, negativity or positivity.

Most people have this thought about money. If I was a millionaire then everything will be fine. I'll be happier. But what if I told you that if I was to give you a million right now? Would you still be the person you are right now or would you be someone different? I think it is safe to say that you will still be the same person you are right now. You will still have these emotions, these feelings and these thoughts. All that's going to change is the digits in your bank account. Yes you might be really overwhelmed and happy to know you are a millionaire, but tomorrow and the day after that and the day after that day, that happiness is slowly going to fade away. You will soon realise it's not what you thought it would be like and that million will soon be gone. After many years that money will eventually disappear as it is not enough. Now you are back to stressing and worrying about your financial future. This is what happens to you when happiness depends on money. What you should do is thinking of ways you can triple that million so you never run out. But at the same time remain humble. Yes money is important especially when you need it to survive and eat. But that does not mean you should be money crazy and forget about what's truly important to you. Don't forget your value!

The reason why I want to be rich is because I want to be able to do the things I love without ever worrying about not having enough money to even eat. I don't want to spend all my time working a job I hate. Money was a big reason why my life was a mess. Because of money I suffered way more then I needed to. So yes believe me I know what's it like, how you will probably give anything to have money. However because I was thinking that way life became even harder. I put money as a first priority and started to think only money and how I can get money. This is selfish. Here is why. When you don't see anything else apart from money being the only thing you ever want, you will lose everything else you had to offer. That could mean you lose your talents, your creativity, your sense of humanity, your kindness, your humbleness and your love for others. When you put money above everything else you are basically saying that you, yourself are not important. You are destroying yourself because you have given pleasure to a materialistic idea.

Be the best version of yourself, focus on that and the money will come chasing you. I want to make a difference and play a big part to society. Every day I constantly set new goals. Yes that means even small goals. Like let me help at least one person today. Even if it's something like helping someone with directions to where they want to go, or giving up my seat to an elderly. Even if I do end up becoming rich I know it's not going to stop there for me. Because with the wealth that I will own, I will set myself a new goal and that will be to help others with my money. Those that need it, like building houses for a small village or paying for someone's medical needs. When we set new goals we will always have something to look forward to. This will help you stay away from depression and worries that you don't need to have in your life. I know that everything is temporary and nothing really matters in the end. I don't need to be stressed about something because I know in the next ten minutes it won't matter. It will be in the past. I live by moments and if a problem occurs in that moment I'll figure out a solution and move on.

If I have a problem with someone I'll speak to them and say this is what I didn't like, instead of having a nonsense argument that will lead to nowhere. I'll talk it out and see what can we do to solve this and where can we go from here.

If something does not go the way I planned no big deal, I'll try something else or try again. Right now I'm in the process of creating something that will be here even long after I'm gone. Even if one person picks up this book and they read it I'll know I've succeeded. I plan to set up multiple businesses in the future that will take our world to a new futuristic place. I also plan to take education to the next level, the fact that you are reading this your educating yourself on how to be successful. All the things I say in this book take notes and try to apply it to your life. I give you permission to copy my ways trust me it works.

I'm always nice to people like I don't get angry that quickly. I have so much patience in anything I do. Yes I'll let you even go in front of me when I'm standing in a long line. Because I know that I won't be here forever. And none of these things will matter. Why should be upset? Why should I run out of patience? Why should I be unhappy? Most importantly why should I spend my time being negative?

Instead I should make the most of my time and be happy, while I'm here. Do the things I love and help those that need me. Life is simple if you make it to be. It all depends on perspective and how your thinking is. Work on your goals and work on your character. The energy you put out there is what you will get in return. I'm proof of that! When I was growing up as a kid I had so many people treated me in the worst way. Even now there are some people who treat me this way. But you know what has changed? Through it all I've always been nice and kind to others. And now that energy that I've constantly put out there has favoured me. I have so many people in my life right now that respect me so much and show so much love. More than I ever asked for!

I have people telling me how I have motivated them, how they are inspired to be better human beings. They all say that I am going to be successful one day. Even though that don't really matter to me what matters to me is that I've become better as a person myself and I've helped others achieve something great! That's true success to me!

I've always had that hunger to achieve greatness. Recently it has just become stronger; I just can't stop now it's become too addicting. I'm addicted to the process of building an empire. I love it! It gives me a rush of energy and motivation I cannot simply ignore. All those nights I stayed hungry and felt nothing but pain made me understand the true meaning of happiness and success. Now I wish to share that with the world!

Why you should never doubt me!

I don't care if it takes me 5 years, 10 years or 30 years as long as god gives me breath for them years, I'm not going nowhere I'm going to keep hustling. I'll never stop. I've been working in silence because soon there is going to come a time where I will no longer need to say anything and my success will make so much noise that everyone has to notice me.

One thing that I learnt is that you have to be consistent with your content. There was so many late nights that I stayed up and just worked. All I wanted to do is just relax and do nothing. I knew that I have to keep going nothing is going to happen magically it's all down to me. I made a lot of sacrifices, instead of doing all the fun things young people my age are doing out there I decided to stay in and work. I rather suffer now then suffer later on in my life.

I've always had that hunger to achieve greatness. Recently it has become stronger; I just can't stop now it's become addicting. I'm addicted to the process of building an empire. I love it. It gives me a rush of energy and motivation to prove to everyone that ever doubted me.

All the anger I feel, all the rage I have I use it as motivation and this is what keeps me going. Having not enough to eat and survive made me get up and do something about. Not doing what I love made me get up and do something about it. No one will be able to stop me no matter how worse my life ends up being. Even if all this does not work out and I end up on the street with nothing, I'll still have everything. Only my creator can stop me, he has written my fate and whatever is meant for me will be mine. It's simple as that so why should I fear the unknown, why should I let failures and people define who I am and what I'm capable of doing. It's all part of the journey. If something goes bad it's because it's meant to for a good reason. If there is someone who is jealous of you and they are trying to ruin everything you have it's because you are doing something right. This is the last thing you should be worried about. No matter what they can't ruin you. Yes they might for the short term but like I said what is meant for you, is meant for you and only you!

There were so many days where I just wanted to give up because nothing was going well for me. No one wanted to listen to what I had to say and no one gave me a chance to show them that I could bring big change. There was no progression happening in my life so many things wasn't going well for me. I was doing everything right delivering content putting myself out there. Nothing was happening, all my hard work and no one here to appreciate it. It is so hard to get yourself heard in today's world especially if you are not someone that is famous or rich. There were so many days where I questioned myself, why am I even doing all this for? My life was going nowhere I was just stuck trying to make things happen. The fact was it wasn't my content, it probably was me, and no one cared about what I had to say mainly because they didn't know who I was. I wasn't a millionaire and I wasn't someone famous, so why would they listen to me! Even if I had life changing words to say. Yes it's sad some people are just like that unfortunately. But that has all changed because you are reading this book now.

I won't be surprised if something does not go well, I mean when it has ever worked out. Nothing is perfect. I'm happy when this happens because it will only make me want it even more. I'm still here aren't I? I'm still working hard and my sense of belief is too strong. I remember one day I and my social worker were talking and we had a really long chat. He said that I have a really strong sense of belief and a drive that is unstoppable. Everyone month that I used to see him I always had something new to tell him about. Always a new update about what's happening in my life. He found that really fascinating and he always used to tell me compare to other people my age I'm doing the most work and actually putting in real effort to achieve success.

Every day I wake up knowing that today could be the day my life changes forever. It is hard to have any hope in our world today, there are so many let downs and so many people out there that will sell you dreams.

Two headed

A: Mitak I told you to stop this nonsense,

They don't care about you & they don't care about your content,

B: but I'm trying to do well and help people, be there for people, we should make it legal,

A: No Mitak it won't work, we tried it before but they left you in the dark,

B: why won't they listen to me?

Maybe because I'm poor but even then I still tried,

A: yes they don't care & they are selfish,

Unless you are rich or famous but for now let's keep it as a wish, and stop being depressed you are hurting your head, you are going to prove them right remember all the things they said?

B: yes I remember I'm a failure & a loser,

A: look I know you got left behind & somehow they blame

you for that & when you are not around they talk behind
your back,

I know they laugh at your life,

They think it's okay,,

The more they laugh at your words

I know the more you are going to use it as a light,

B: I don't even know why I make this stuff for people to
see,

I rather make a video of me bashing my head on a wall,
because people rather watch that then watch a life
changing advice from me,

So many people hurt me and I'm still waiting on my time, I

want to take their eyes out and stuff it in their ears, or even shoot through their nose till it comes out their skull,

A: wow Mitak stop talking like that, we know you are mad, all the anger and rage has made you a psychopath, all the people that have hurt you including your dad,

That Aunty that kept you she is even worse, she kept you away from your mum, she could have done something about that,

B: and all them fake people I know who they are, I'm coming for them I'm about to mess their whole life up, I want them to beg me and cry and say sorry for the wrong they did to me,

A: Mitak they going to get what they deserve, people are

not that nice out there, don't you remember the girl you
liked and she couldn't even reply to your text,

B: oh yeah I remember that, I feel like strangling her with
her own hair strand, like how dare she do that to me? If
only she knew who I am going to be! Ha,

A: okay relax, we all know you have been through a lot,
and there is a monster inside you that you cannot fix,

We know you feel messed up; we know you feel dead, we
know you want to shoot someone in the head,

B: I wanted people to understand my story, but they judge
way before they even listen to a word I have to say,

A: Mitak I know this frustrates you, and I know it might be too late to bring you back, but I know there is good in you please just give them one more chance, I know you are thinking I can't wait to prove them wrong,

I know all you ever wanted was to become successful so you can show everyone how you did it,

Even them fake friends have hurt you, after all they said you just feel like cutting their tongues,

You no longer fear death as you welcome it, but please Mitak don't lose yourself to the dark side, you are your own brand believe in it that,

B: No! They won't listen any more, it's too late for that,

I've gone beyond a point where I can no longer come back, and it was all because of them they didn't give me a chance to show who I really am, now I must destroy what was once a quiet place in my quiet mind.

A: You can change for the better or you can change for the worse, choose wisely because whatever you choose that will be your path,

B: okay I understand I guess I give it another try, maybe I don't have it in me to change for the worse, but I know one thing I'll never give up on this success path,

A: yes now that's more like the Mitak I know, just be you and watch people will soon notice your good work!

B: yes I need to put my emotions aside & think about all the good I can do with my life,

So here I come, here I rise, and I have chosen the good because this is right.

I wrote this when I was going through a point in my life, where I had two options to either carry on being me or go bad and be something I don't like. I was doing everything right trying to make a change and motivate others with my words. I started documenting everything that was going on in my life so people could see how I have changed my life around. I wanted people to see the journey I've been through and currently going through. But I felt like my work wasn't being appreciated by anyone.

Nobody wanted to watch any of my videos because it was

too boring or shall I say too real. All those days I was creating content and putting it out there for the world to see and take something from it, not a single person even said to me what I'm doing is amazing and it will change lives.

It was so frustrating and demotivating because I felt like I was wasting my time. I have all these good fruitful knowledge to give but there was no one at the end of it to receive it. I was going nowhere with this, wasn't making any progress. At that time so much happened. There were a lot of people that hurt me and let me down. I was desperate to make things happen.

I was looking for just one opportunity to just really show who I am. I'm that sort of person that takes every opportunity I get. I really just wanted to give up quit YouTube and quit social media. But I realised that things like this takes time, a lot of time. You can't expect to be an overnight success and you can't expect for things to magically happen. Even with my business I was struggling a lot. I wasn't getting the attention I deserved.

Then I discovered Garyvee, he showed what true hustle

should look like. For over 10 years he has been making content and putting it out there. I started watching all his old videos from 2008 till now. Wow it was amazing, I can see the hunger he had and the grind was so real. Watching his video I learnt so many things. Document everything.

You have to be consistent with your content. Never giving up no matter how bad things may get.

I remember this one video that I watched and it was really inspiring when a little girl asked Gary vee a question about being a YouTuber. What Gary said was perfect for me. He said that it will take so much time and for the next few years don't even worry about how many subscribers or likes or comments you have. He also said that nobody was watching him for a long time until just recently he became popular. But it took him all these years to build himself up and build a good personal brand for himself.

At that point I realised if I wanted to build my own personal brand I needed to do exactly what Gary did. I wanted to make sure I work so hard that I will always be delivering content no matter what. I forced myself into a habit that soon became really addicting for me. I ended up having so much discipline that any time I was not working I would feel guilty. If I started playing a game or watching anime I would stop straight away because I would feel guilty of not doing work. I would feel like I am falling behind.

However after I do my work and when I feel like I've done enough for today then I could finally relax and watch anime. I love anime! Even till this day I watch anime. I've even been collecting all the manga (comic book) from different anime.

No I am not a machine and I'm not telling you to work yourself to death. But you should always put work as a high priority. After you feel satisfied with what you have achieved today, then relax. Make sure you always remember to take small breaks. The more breaks you take the better. It will help you stay productive and you won't lose focus. Don't stay in the same place, go somewhere else from where you were working. Anyway I think I went off topic a bit but back to the point what I'm trying to say is that your work ethic is really important especially if you want things to happen.

I saw the things Gary was doing and I thought you know what I could do that! In fact I need to do that in order to achieve my goals. So I began to work hard and although I am not there I know one day I will be there.

I'm not mad at you

I guess you was the father figure to me,

Even though my dad wasn't around,

you was always there for me,

I'll never forget the days you cared for me,

It's been so long since you left me,

I remember them times when we used to sit there alone,

Talk about all the things that are right and wrong,

You never liked it when I sat and cried,

And you knew for a fact I wasn't a happy child,

So you used to take me out used to take me far,

take me to all these places just to heal my scars,

You knew I was a lost child looking for his mum,

I knew you didn't want to keep me

Because you saw the way it was hurting me,

But still somehow you tried to fight for me,

You tried to give me a happy childhood,

You tried so bad,

I was like a son that

You never had,

I remember them times you was like,

As long as I'm happy then your okay,

I never saw you after that

That was the last time I saw you,

When you was in hospital,

And it was your last moments

You just wanted to see me before you went,

But I was too angry to come

See you one last time,

Now I realised that

You was the only one that truly understood my life,

And every time I got in trouble

You always took my side,

My biggest regret is

Not coming to say a last goodbye,

But I know if you were still here you would say,

To keep moving forward and learn from my mistakes,

I remember you used to make me breakfast

And always fixed me a plate,

Every time you sat to eat

you made sure I sat with you and ate,

I guess I was just mad at the world

And everything it did to me,

You saw the rage in my eyes

And that's why you always advised me,

You told me to do what I love

And be able to

Tell the difference between

A good & a bad friend,

All I want to say now is forgive me

And I'm sorry for everything,

Thank you for everything

And I'm not mad at you.

-Dedicated to Soloman Makaddar (the man who raised me)

Soloman Makaddar, he was a man of few words. We wasn't related by blood but you took care of me like I was part of your DNA. From the start when I first came to your house at the age of six, you didn't want to take me. Not because you didn't care but because you knew what awaits me. You knew all the nights I will struggle and miss my parents. You always wanted nothing but good for me, I knew the love you had for me was real. All the sacrifices you made I didn't realise till I was way older, it was as if you was the one that was working all this magic in the background. Silently making sure I was always happy.

Every time you used to sit to eat, you will always call me to come eat with you. Even when you made breakfast I'll be there enjoying the meal with you. People might think well this is not something big, but believe me for me this meant a lot. Just these small actions meant a lot to me at that time and even till this day. It is the small actions that have a huge impact and meaning.

We used to go out to all these different places, I mean the only reason I know all these cool places to go to in London is because of you. We went arcade, boat riding, to the zoo, funfair, museums, cinema, you name it! I remember one day we went to this gaming launch near Trafalgar square. There was all of these games, Xbox and Playstation was also there. There were holding a Fifa tournament as well and I took part, I lost big time but I mean for a nine year old I did pretty good wining all these goodies.

I also remember when you introduced me to Michael

Jackson in 2008 just a year before he died. You had all his songs and used to play them on the CD player, before all this tech came out.

I appreciate everything you have done for me, the way you raised me. I didn't have my father and I was always looking for that figure. I soon realised I didn't need my father because I had you. You did so much for me way more then my real father can imagine. I didn't want money or anyone to buy me stuff and give me things to make me forget my pain. I needed love, guidance, someone I can talk to about what's bothering me, someone who will listen more then trying to tell me to grow up and that everything will be okay. Someone that will go places with me, someone who can show me how to be a man, how to be a good human, how to take care of people, how a father should be like. That's what I needed, and you showed me all of that. You didn't have to say anything but spending time with you I gained knowledge that you didn't have to teach me. Like how to be a good father, how to love your wife and kids and like what really matters in this world.

Your examples showed me being healthy, having

patience and being wise will take you to far places.

The last time I saw you was on the train after I left the house and came into care. I thought you would be angry but you seemed relief like you understood why I left. In fact you was the only person who understood. You told me to call you and speak to you on the phone even if I don't speak to my aunty, at least speak to you. You just wanted to know if I was okay, if I ate, if I needed anything you will be there even if it meant secretly meeting up with me. That's how much you cared. But I was too angry to realise what you was trying to tell me at the time and I didn't listen. Wow this is so hard for me to write, I'm filled with emotions right now...

The last thing you said to me was, "no matter what you do, as long as you are happy I am happy." I never saw you after that.

Few months later you fell ill and was in hospital, you kept asking for me. You kept asking everyone to see me. But I never came. Then soon later you passed away, the news hit me, I was shocked and broke down. I realised that this world is temporary, holding grudges, being angry with people and being stubborn will only destroy yourself. It will make you have regrets. You don't know who will be here today and who won't be tomorrow. Make sure the last thing you say to someone is loving and kind. Otherwise you will have regrets eating you away.

That's exactly what's happening to me. For many days I sat the whole night crying because I didn't get to say goodbye and thank you. Now I will never know what he wanted to say to me in his last moments, I let him leave him in a state of worry for me instead of letting him go with a hug and letting him know how much I appreciate him.

Now everything seems like it's all falling apart. I don't have my father any more and my inspiring role model that I will always remember for the rest of my life.

I just want to say I am sorry, please forgive me and thank you for everything.

I just wanted to make you proud, I wanted you to be here watch me become successful. Watch me buy my first big house, be there at my wedding, meet your grandchildren and see the man I become that you raised.

I wanted to write more memories but I'm going to be selfish here and not mention them. I'll just keep them to myself so I can cherish them, only I know them.

Well I guess I'll see you on the other side, just wait for me. We can sit and drink whatever you drink over there, I'll tell you all the stories of this life and most importantly I'll tell you how I missed you every time and always kept you in mind everyday no matter what I did. I know all the blessings and all these good things that are happening in my life is because you and god are watching me. I can't wait to see you one day. I hope you are happy up there and I pray for you everyday.

I miss you, thank you and I'm sorry.

To the man who raised me- Soloman Makaddar.

Where I am right now in my life- 2019

I used the year 2018 to just build myself up and really work on my goals. By the time 2018 ended I had launched a Digital Marketing company. Came up with few business ideas that I could start in a few years, if this does not work out. Soon as I launched I was so excited, I have finally finished the website and creating materials to put on my social media sites. What made it hard for me was that I was doing everything by myself. No one would be willing to help me. Well that for free. Nothing is free nowadays which is a shame because it shows how much love we have for money rather than for humans.

Every move that I have made has been a calculated step to take me closer to my death. I talk about death like it is the best thing that can happen to you. People look at me like I am psycho and maybe I am. I am cursed and this is the only thing I look forward to. I am suicidal so be careful but at the same time I love life so that stops me.

I felt like I was in jail sitting in a cell for crime I did not commit. When I used to live in a room all I ever saw was these four walls and a medium sized window with the ugliest view. I spent a lot of time with my thoughts. It gave so much time to think about things that not many people have time to think about. I knew this was a game changer for me because everything I was feeling at that time and all my thoughts was so powerful I had to write it down. Well, all those things are the things you are reading about now in this book. I stopped writing my book I just gave up with it I thought this was too dark and serious no one will read it. Until a few people read it and some of them cried, some of them said I'll never take life for granted and some of them said they are so thankful that I didn't end my life. They are so thankful that there is someone like me in the world that exists. They told me that I should go ahead and finished this because it is so powerful and meaningful. It will change lives. At that moment I knew why I sat alone all those nights and why my mind was begging to explode with creativity. It was for those reactions I wanted people to have that reaction every time they read this book. And they can keep going back to this book every time their life went downhill. Every time I was out I would tell people or even my friends that you see that book shop? My book will be there one day. Or you see that big screen over there my face will be there. My book will be on everyone's shelves and it will help people change theirs and also someone else's lives. That is one of my goals for 2019.

I hope to finish this book and publish this book. I also want my business to just take off. I know 2019 is not my year it is too soon. 2020 or 2021 might be my year if my creator gives me breath for another few years.

Right now I am still working my part time job as well as working on building this business and writing this book. I've a lost a lot friends but it is fine I've been focused on my making a difference. I stopped talking to a lot of people and I've just been quiet. I am working silence and being really patient. I come from work and I am still working just to make my dreams come true. I don't know when the last time I went shopping for myself or even treated myself. I can't even sit and play games because I have that constant thought and feeling that I am falling behind and I need to get back to work. I am working on building my personal brand and start my journey to becoming one of the top motivational and life changing humans to ever exist!

I am currently in the process of building a team with my best friend and mentor Emmanuel. I have been trying to do everything myself and that has put more stress and pressure on me. This did not help either because I was getting nowhere. Now we are building a loyal team that are not just helping me out but we are all helping each other out. The reason why me and Emmanuel decided to build a team it was so that everyone in the group can help each other with their skills as well as work on our own things and get help if we need. Now everyone in our team had different roles and skills they can bring to the table as well as give us a chance to sponge of each other and take some ideas.

Hopefully this will give me some space to breathe and really get my head in the right space because right now my mind is all over the place. Right now I have all these amazing ideas but I think I need to slow down a little and take it one idea at a time.

A lot people always say to me Mitak you need to relax and just stop here and there. Mitak you are only 20 years and we know you are way ahead of your time especially from those that are your age. But you need to life happen and go as each day comes. I knew at that moment that some of those things they said was actually true and right. Maybe I am rushing it and going too fast. But the thought of me falling behind or wasting my time just gives me an adrenaline to not stop. I feel like other people that are my age and those that are in my generation are moving ahead of me and they are becoming successful. And I'm here not doing anything.

But when I gave it some thought I realised that it was actually the other way around. When I spoke to someone my age they are unable to keep up with what I'm saying or what I am doing because I'm thinking in a completely different dimension. They are unable to understand what my visions are because they are not thinking like me. That is why so many of my friends don't even want to get involved with me or with any of the business ideas that I have. Which is a shame. This lead to me loosing touch with them and I just begun to distance myself from them. I started surrounding myself with more people that were thinking like me or similar to me.

A lot the young generation they are not thinking about how they can change their lives and become better. Or how they can start their journey towards success. They are all waiting for when they turn 30 or 35 years old and realise that this is not the life they want. They are not happy and now they want to start their own business and be free.

At that time they will be in a huge disadvantage which is they might not having many years to actually make that happen as they are growing old. But then again it is never too late. But what I am trying to say is that imagine that you started this at 20 instead of 30, you will now be 10 years ahead of doing what you love and enjoy. Maybe you might even retire at 30 because you have reached your success.

Young people nowadays are thinking about who the next top artist is, what is the next new shoes that will come out, what new car I can hire so I can impress some girls and show off or what is the next day that I can go out partying with my friends. The list goes on!

If you are a young person or someone that is growing old whoever you may be, know that it is still not too late. You can change your life and do what you want. Yes it will mean hard nights and a lot of sacrifices. But that will be worth it. The reason why you are reading this book right now? Is a sign that you want something. Maybe you were looking for a way you can change your life, maybe you wanted some motivation, maybe you wanted to a little push, maybe you wanted some words to tell you straight in the face, wake up, stop wasting time doing pointless things and do something with the gift you have been given, meaning life.

It is June now of 2019, and finally a lot of things are starting to go my way for once. I am getting more opportunities and I am getting more people contacting me to work with me. Some of them even want me as their business partners, like what an honour! I am so thankful. The creepy thing is when I said I will have multiple businesses in the future? I am starting to see that happening right now. Like it is just starting that phase of my life. It is crazy how life works. I just hope it carries on like this and everyday I pray for this blessing to stay and for my creator to continue to make me a better person.

Don't count on anyone

I changed my ways,
I took control of things,

The day they doubted me
Was the day I stopped counting on anyone,

Living in a room,
Concealed by my own issues,
I went and got what I deserve,
Been working the grind didn't stop,

Since early I've been married to the game,
Now I want a divorce,
Me and her are having too many
Disagreements,

Tired of let downs
Tried of disappoints,
Only make time for those who are worth it,
Looks like we need to make Appointments,

Make a master plan watch the return blow up,
Make a masterpiece watch it last forever,
I'm pro gifted I'm pro talented,
I'm pro everything that the world told me I am not,,

I been doing it on my own,
No handouts and no support,
I do it like it's the only thing I own,
I do it like it's the only way,

All alone,

They are not seeing it now
but soon they will,
They don't believe now,
But soon this will be what they believe in,

Sitting on the step feeling no feelings,
Seeing all these kind of visions,
Waiting for my mum to come,
But that's something I'm not seeing,

Sitting on the step waiting for the time go,
The rage and hunger
Mixed with patience,
Gave me this flow,

Don't care any more who is with me &
Who is not,
I'm headed towards the end
Without any means,

I'm at the point of no return
And that's how I like it,
I'm living on a rope
About to end it,

Everyone in my business
Like I'm wanted,
But before I leave
I'll save everyone that's stranded,

I changed my ways,
I took control of things,
The day they doubted me
Was the day I stopped counting on anyone,

Questions

When you think about it questions are a crucial element to the human mind. Imagine we didn't have this as a brain cell. How lost the world would be. No, more like how zombie like and dead people will be. Because of questions we have ideas and inventions. We have innovations that we never thought would be possible. We as humans will completely loose the purpose of life if we were not able to question anything.

It is good to question everything. Why do you think little kids tend to ask you a lot of questions? Yes most of it comes from their desperate search for discovery, creativity and from them being really curious about learning whatever they can get their hands on. But the other reason is because they need answers in order to develop and grow. Just like that we never stop asking questions. We as humans are a curious creation and we are constantly looking to learn new things and look for new possibilities.

Imagine the person who created electricity never asked a question of why couldn't we have a device that provided light also knows as a light bulb in today's world. Or imagine if Newton never questioned gravity. How would the world be like now?

What if all those people that discovered different types of materials and those people that discovered technology, never asked questions. Would we still have nice buildings to live in? Or would we have something called the internet? Or even a computer?

So in same way you should be asking yourself questions everyday about your life and about what you want to do in the future. Even with your business ask yourself, why do I want to do this? How should I go about doing this? What is it that I am truly after? Well you get the picture right?

Asking questions is the only way we all can move forward, because it helps us come up with answers that help us live as humans. If someone is telling you something yes listen, but ask questions. Question things like what if this was like this or what if this could be like this. Without the need to find answers we would be just blank. Imagine there was people out there that had no idea what they want to do in life or they don't know what they love doing. I mean even in our world today there are some people who don't know what they love or know what they want to do in life which is okay. But not knowing for too long is a bad thing. We should have at least one or two ideas about what we like to do even if later we realise it is not the one. It is all bout failing, trial and error.

But the minute we question ourselves especially when life puts us in a difficult situation that is when the best version of us emerges. Like me when I was working a job I hated, I realised and asked myself a very important question which changed a lot of things for me. That question was 'do I really want to be doing this for the rest of my life?' This really made me think about everything and most importantly I questioned my values. I felt like I was in an interrogation room interviewing myself one side determined to know the answer and the other side anxious and worried about what that answer will be.

I soon begun to get few job offers but it was too late for me, my mind was in a different space now. It was almost as if I felt I was too good enough to be just working a normal job for the rest of my life. All of a sudden I wanted more out of life because I felt like I could do way more if I was living on my terms. This all happened simply because I questioned myself, and more like questioned my values. I felt unstoppable like I can conquer anything. I've been jobless for so long that it pushed me to develop myself into something where I would no longer need a job. Now I can see that everything does happen for a reason. If I ended up just getting a job and working I would have never started my own business, I would have never picked up a book or a camera and record my life and even would have never wrote this book for you. Now are we glad that didn't happen? Because I'm certainly glad! That Is why I am thankful for everything I have ever been through in my life. Even though I would want that steady job and income, I knew that wasn't me. I could do so much more by being me and by being free and doing what I love and enjoy.

So make sure you question yourself and everything you do in life. Question it and ask yourself why are doing this? What is it that you truly want? What would make you happy? What does the perfect life look like to you? Is this the right thing for you to do? Are you currently happy? If not why are you not happy? And what can change that? So you will be happy.

Always be Real

One thing that I always tell myself? Is that no matter what I do in life or who I aim to be, I'm always going to be real. By that I mean I'm always going to be me. Even if I'm emailing a potential client that could just change my life or even if I have to send an email that could decide whether I have a million pound deal or not. I'll always be real. It's a big risk I know, but if people don't like it then they can buzz off.

Even if it means I'll lose the deal. I'm not going to pretend to be someone I am not and I'm not going to act or talk professionally just to give a good impression. No instead I'm going to be myself. I'll introduce myself in that email to you in the most raw and powerful way because that's the only way I know how to. Ever since I was young that's all I've been doing. Is being real. I talk about my past like it's my greatest achievement. I talk about my struggles like it's my greatest accomplishments. I say all of these things to let you know that I'm no ordinary person, I'm extraordinary and you will be a fool to not have me in your life. Like I tell people recognise the people who can make a difference to you. That means surrounding yourself with those who uplift you to do better. If I just sent you a boring email trying to persuade you to buy my products or services how likely are you going to reply to that email?

But what if I sent you an email that really had your face expression like wow! And it was just few lines about me who I am where I come from and who I want to be. I tell you the deepest heart touching sentences as well as a motivational line that makes you feel good about reading this email. I just simply end the email with my intentions no lies the truth simple and clean. If my intention is I want you to be my client I'll let you know that in the email. If I want you to invest in my business I'll also tell you that. Straight and clean with honestly and realness. I guarantee you that you will hit that reply button ASAP!

What if I sent you something like this...

Hi (name)

Hope you are well,

I'm Mitak nice to meet you. Let me just tell you a bit about myself.

After graduating a 4 years self development programme from the age of 15 to the age of 18, and as a Care leaver I have now started a digital marketing company and currently writing one of the most motivational and life changing book that will be published soon! I have turned my life around. I'm on the road to success and I have already achieved a lot by the age of 20. I now plan to set up multiple businesses in the future as well as publish more books and become one of the top motivational speakers to ever exist. I believe that whatever struggle I've been through since I was a child to now it's all for a reason, to help and make a huge difference in the world. I believe my work, my words and my experiences can do exactly that!

The reason for me sending you this email is that I really love what you are doing and I would love to work with you. I provide a digital marketing service to businesses in London and I would really want you to be my client. I would love to explain this to you further.

Why don't we have a chat maybe on the phone or over a cup of coffee?

Looking forward to hearing from you,

Kind regards,
Mitak Ahmed.

Now a lot of people won't be used to these kind of emails. Nowadays emails and letters just seem so scripted and boring. Unfortunately people are used to this and they think that the scripted old fashioned way of writing is acceptable. So when they see an email like this? They straight away shut it down and think it's too unprofessional. When matter of fact this type of email is making you look even more professional. The fact that you was able to say something about yourself to a complete stranger shows power and confidence. The fact that you was able to step out of your comfort zone and talk about something you was once uncomfortable to talk about. You kept it real about who you are and you told them clearly what your intentions are. This is way more professional then anything else. It shows you have humbleness, honesty, confidence in who you are and what you do, belief in yourself and shows that you are not afraid to speak about your past weaknesses. You are also able to show how those weaknesses has become one of your strongest points. Believe me there are so many people who would love to read an email like this. You will be surprised trust me.

Always be yourself and real. Because you never know what you will get. But by being real you are showing that you are in control, you have high sense of belief, you have self discipline, morals and respect for yourself.

There is no fake it till you make it here. If you are just starting out then it's okay. You don't have to pretend that you have a lot of money and already successful. Be real! Yes be real. It's okay if you don't have all the answers. You will be happy to know no one does!

You'll meet so many people that act like they have it all figured out but truly they don't. No one does. Yes you might listen to someone that is a millionaire and take advice from them. But after that it all comes down to you. Everyone is living in different dimensions in the same world. Everyone is going through their own journey. So depending on what journey you are currently on? You need to take that advice and make it your own. See how that can apply to you.

Throughout this book you will see that I repeat a lot of things and that because I really want that to stick in your head so you don't forget it after you close this book.

So I'll end this by saying...

'Being real is the best brand you can be.'

Dark days & rain

Right now I look at my life
Like a maze & a scribbled page,
They will never take me alive
I'll always stand by what I love,

I'll never stop fighting for my rights,
I may never see true peace,
But I swear I will die
before I let a man tell me how to live life,

Sometimes I think does she really love me,
Or is she just by my side
Till the time comes for her to leave & betray me,
Issues & doubts so I need constant reassurance,

But no worries one day I'll be gone
& none of this will matter,

Now everyone I meet has something to prove,
Like yeah they the big man
And they act like they know it all,
I wasn't so lucky & I had no choice,

It makes me sick seeing people take things for
Granted,

I hustle with no plug,
I motivate like there is no tomorrow,
I have no fear & I fear no one,
Only the being that made this soul,

Burn my emotions & burn my feelings,
Fuming with anger & rage,
Just cut the small talks
It's all the same,

They got me going crazy & insane,
They tell me I'm the cure & the saviour for this place,
I'm not free I've been in prison
Waiting for my bail,
So everyday I make it rain
& let this rain wash away this pain.

Don't be afraid of death

Don't be afraid of death and don't be afraid to live. Be
afraid that you will lose you trying to figure life out. Just
live and be happy with what you have. Everything is

temporary don't take everything so seriously and don't run away from what's bothering you. This pain you feel now show love to it because it made you who you are. It is making you better think of it as an upgrade. You are levelling up to go to the next level. So don't be so focused on this life that you forget what's really important, YOU!

Mum If you are reading this then just know that I was never happy here. This world is not for me. But I still tried to make things work and be someone you can be proud of. When I leave this place just remember I was someone that cared about others more then myself. I love people and being there to help people in any way I can. I wanted to help people change their ways and become better humans. And if anyone that is reading this and you knew me or know of me, then remember me in the right way. When someone asks about me speak about who I was and what I believed in. Tell them that life is nothing but a passing journey. It's not permanent. Nothing is! The reason why I'm doing all of this is so that it can help people. And oh yeah tell them that I was one motivational and unstoppable soul!

I started off with chasing success and everything that was in this world. I soon realised that I thought this would give me happiness but I know it won't. The only reason I wanted to be successful is so that I can live in this world peacefully and just survive till my time came.

If today my creator gave me two options, to go and be with him or to carry on living here and he'll make me rich, even live like a king. I would choose to be with him. Because no richness can compare to my creator and why try live like a king when you can be with a king. The king of all kings!

I knew that my happiness wasn't in this world, it never even existed in this world all this time. I just thought it did. My happiness was with my creator. So until then I must do whatever it takes to make sure he is happy to see me when I finally meet him. Yes that means being good in this world, caring for humans and leaving behind something others can benefit from.

I carry a lot of pain and a lot of dark thoughts but at the same time a lot of goodness that can turn those negatives around. Mum I know you struggled so much and you know I did too. I wish I could write about happy things but there is so much things wrong with this world that I can't.

When I was little all I cared about is being with my parents and with my family. Even if I was living on the streets none of those things mattered as long as I had my family. That shows I don't care about money or whatever this false image of living the good life is. I always knew that tomorrow I might not be here so why I should I worry about those things? Being successful is being you! The real you! When you figure who you really are and when you can be you freely without worrying about what the world will judge you as. It's about standing for who you are and what you believe, sticking to your values.

Don't change for others and don't change yourself to please others. Success is always there, anyone can have it. The reason why most people are not is because they lack the vision to see it. Life and hardships block us from seeing it. Why do you think a lot of people just give up and live a life they are not happy with. The same old boring job and the same old routine. You need to open your mind and see past the illusion, that success is hard. Success is what you make it out to be. Till this day there is no certain definition of what success is, because everyone has their own definition of success.

That means it is entirely up to you. You are in charge of your life and what success you need to be happy. If success to you is living in a small house and living the simple peaceful life? Then do that! That's perfect! But if success is a luxury lifestyle you desire then you need to do that. One mistake I see people making is that they think they will be happy once they have those things or they will be happy once they are successful. This is wrong! You need to be happy now. In this current moment you are in, you need to be happy with that. Then only will you be able to be truly happy. It's all about the present moment you are living in. The Present moment is certain, but the future is uncertain. Because you might not be here tomorrow. So live for today, that's the only way you can move forward to achieving what you want!

'Feel alive, be alive and live.'

Flashback

Throughout it all I know I'm going to look back at my life and just laugh. I can't believe I got through what I went through, I can't believe I did it. Even writing this book it just started one day when I was sitting in front of a laptop wondering what to do. I just started writing and well, here I am. I knew there was something missing, like I always had so much to say. I was looking for something or somewhere, a platform that I can say everything that is inside. But most importantly talk about my life and share my story with the world. Well I found a platform, writing this book, my podcast called Mitak's incomplete and making videos on YouTube and everywhere. At first writing about my life felt really weird. However over time it got easier and I loved it. I finally found a place where I can let off some steam. Not just fighting or hitting the gym but actually writing. Could you believe that? I mean come on, when was the last time you heard someone say, I am going to let off some steam by writing. It's insane and strange. Yes that is what a lot people thought. I changed that perspective completely once people read the type of content I am writing about. They understood what I meant by letting off some steam.

I soon realised that writing is my passion and it is something I love doing. Creative writing is what I enjoy and can just sit there all day and just write. I plan to write plenty more books in the future. It will be fantasy type books, mystery and anything my creative cortex can think of. I just can't wait! Soon as I am done with this book I am starting on a new fantasy book that I hope to eventually create into an anime. Yes you heard, an ANIME!

Actually I just had a great idea, maybe I can also do creative writing/ story writing for films, anime, cartoons, video games and even shows. Now ain't that a thought?

Now I'm telling you I have so much to offer to the world, even I don't know where all this will take me. All I know is that something amazing awaits me. And oh yeah the best part is, I'm not even thinking about the money. But if you want to talk about the money? I'll tell you now there is no doubt that I will be rich. Whether your talking materialism or having something money can't buy? I will be rich.

I know in the future I will look back at this and I will be so thankful I wrote this book. Like sometimes I think I'm just crazy, like how did I do this. I never thought I will be able to achieve what I achieved.

My flashbacks used to be about my past, my struggles, now the flashbacks is going to be about me writing this book and about this journey I went through.

Kindred Soul

Look in to the future,
look in my eyes,
You can see the hunger,
You can see my life,

Just don't fall in love,
Just don't fall for my heart,

my heart is not like my mind,
You might feel good or you might cry,
Yesterday you was okay,
Today you are fine,

Let's slow it down,
Let's take our time,
Why you always in a rush,
Take it slow let's be patient,

Come walk this path with me,
Come build this empire with me,
Let me take you to any place you wish,
Come share this love stop being selfish,

We can sit near the waterfall,
Or we can dream in the clouds,
Blind sanity and trust issues,
Makes me regret and have doubts,

My diamonds and my jewels are not clean,
But you can be the miracle that will shine,
I've always had the treasure,
You just never noticed,

Through the miseries, through the pain,
Through the heartbreaks, through the love game,
Let me get lost with your soul,
Slowly and slowly conquering everything,

I know I'll die alone but still I'm hoping,
Maybe I'm lost, maybe I'm crazy with no hope,
Maybe all this was so I can be with you,

Or maybe this was just another imagination,

I know it is better in heaven,
I know its us I believe in,
I know it is me you want to be loving,
And I know this world is something we can't live in,

I'm sitting on this throne knowing I won this fight,
Because with you I know,
There is nothing I can't face,
So take your time and step this way,

Sometimes it hurts,
Sometimes it burns,
When you don't see that
All I want is your love,

I can see the energy we have,
The dancing cells,
The dancing strings of emotions,
Fill our emptiness,

I can see the pictures flash by,
The past running trying to be by your side,
It says your the future,

Be forever more with your smile,

This is how love should sound like,
The feeling that there is another soul that wants you,
If I opened my world,
Showed you my mind,
Maybe you will think I'm a psycho,
Maybe you will know how to love me right,

I'm just waiting for my time to die,
Yes I'm crazy and suicidal,
But that means you need to be my reason
To live,
And I'll love hard,

Come be the one I can deep it to,
That we can go places where our mind can't find,
Let's explore this efficacious love,
Lets share these broken secrets,

Look in to the future,
look in my eyes,
You can see the hunger,
You can see my life,

Just don't fall in love,
Just don't fall for my heart.

Yours Truly

To all the women of this world, here is a humble request from yours truly. Please find yourself a man that knows how to treat you right. I'm tired of seeing these guys mistreating women and then these same women go with the same type of men.

To all the men of this world here is also a humble request from yours truly. Find yourself a strong, sensible and caring woman. Look for a woman that just doesn't respect herself or you, but she respects "us".

Find someone that you will be happy with, not have constant arguments, fights, jealousy, trust issues or problems. Now if you are thinking well this is impossible because relationships nowadays like this does not exist any more, then that means you have been in the wrong relationship this whole time. We only talk from experience that means you just had bad experiences with relationships in the past. Trust me I have been in one or two of those too.

Maybe you both just need to stop playing games and be honest with each other. Or maybe you just need to let each other know what you want and what you expect from being in this relationship with them. And if the answer is not something like the poem you just read (kindred soul) then you need to get up and leave. Move on, focus on yourself and when the time is right, the right one will be in your presence.

Relationships have never been for me. Every time I use to hear that I ran the other way. Like why can't I just love you without us putting a label or tag on it. You know what I am saying? I did go with the completely wrong females I have to admit. Well I was young and naive. I always thought the problem was them, but it was me. One, I didn't know what I want and two, I was on a mission. There was even times when I wanted to sit on my throne with my future wife, and there was times where I just needed to complete my mission and leave this place. So there was no point being in a relationship if I am not going to be around.

But love being the powerful emotion that it is, it has made it hard for me not to fall in love. I mean I am in love with the future wife that will come into my life soon. Yes I am crazy and revolutionary. Anyway you get what I mean love is not a skill you can learn, it just happens. I am no expert but from seeing my mothers relationship with my dad and even from my personal experience I can say I know how love is supposed to be like. I know how to treat women in the right way. And yes damn right I'll treat my wife in a way she will feel like she owns this world and everything in it. Even though I know that we will both just be happy that we have each other. I see life and everything as moments and stages. Right now I know I am at a stage where I am building myself up. I am not ready for that stage to be in love. I know that moment will come and that is whole new different journey itself. Currently I am trying to finish this stage I am on now. But as soon as my future wife enters my life I know that this stage has ended and it is now time for to enter the new journey. I am actually excited and looking forward to it.

So yes this could mean she comes tomorrow then that is it my new stage has begun. That does not mean my mission and goals stop, just means I have someone that will ride with me till the end. So make sure you are with the right person and make sure that you enjoy every moment with them. Time goes too quick before you know it you both will be old.

Underestimate

Over the years as I was growing up I saw a lot people talk a big game but have never followed through.

They all spoke like they knew it all and like they knew what they were talking about. These are the sort of people that thought they are better than you, like they are superior to you. I was always failing at everything I was doing. Even though at that time I was only a child and you would think well it's okay if you fail your just a kid. But that was not the problem. I know through out this book I always speak about how I need to prove people wrong and how I always feel like a failure. It is because I was at a point and a place in my life where I believed this to be the truth. I told myself that this is me, this is who I am.

I spent most of my time listening to people labelling me to who I am. Me and Identity have always been in conflict. A war between two nations. I might have won the battle at the time but I guess I was fighting on my own, where as identity had some back up from all the people that were putting a label on me.

People doubt me and judge me really quick. But what they fail to understand is I am that sort of person that won't show you who I am straight away. I observe people and learn what their behaviours, personality and what kind of person they are. Because I have been doing this constantly over the years, I have developed a skill that I didn't even know I had. I am able to read people, the way people talk and their body language tells me a lot. The way someone complains and the type of words they use in their speech, says a lot. People don't realise but they give out more signals than they realise. I learnt this power (sounds better than skill) by letting people take advantage of me. Yes I failed at school and technically at everything I did, but that gives you no right to label me and tell me I will not be able to achieve anything in my life.

I remember the time where I use to stay in a room. It was a house where other young boys like me was staying. We all had our own room but we had to share the kitchen and the bathroom. I went to this place after I turned 18 and after my foster parents house. This was before I got my place. I stayed at this place for 2 years. Yes that means staying in that one room, with nothing but a small fridge, cupboard, a single bed, a small table and a 14 inch small TV. I had a lot of trust issues and I always use to lock my room, even when I went to the bathroom. Well if you had to keep moving about, meeting new people all the time and unsure where your life is heading. You will also have a lot of issues and problems.

A feeling of constant stress, uncertainty, rage and

feeling like your safety is always at threat. I spent a lot of nights here thinking about what I should do, and I think this was my time where I changed. I was developing myself, it was like my time where I had nothing but time to reflect and think. I was levelling up. upgrading to something amazing. I took everything I learnt and I took all of the negativity people have been giving to me over the years and used it as fuel. For so days all I saw was these 4 walls and my visions for the future. I saw my goals and ambitions playing out over and over again, till it was engraved with my brains cells. All of a sudden I felt a sensation of mercy and blessing from my creator. As if he was trying to show me a way out. Well after all he is the only one that has seen me in my darkest moments and knows exactly what I am going through. It was at this moment, everything became more real to me. Achieving success, knowing that there is more to my life than this and knowing that success can be achieved with my creators support.

I also spent a lot of time thinking about what kind of person would I be in the future, or more like who I would be. Will I be happy? Will I be someone strong, powerful and inspiring? Will be one of the greatest? After I die will I leave a legacy behind for people to follow?

They say over thinking is bad, I say it depends on what you are over thinking about. Because believe me the things I was over thinking about were things you just read about, and look where it got me. It created amazing opportunities and opened so many doors for me. It even got me writing this book for you, so hopefully this book can help you and people who read this. This room that I was living in felt like a prison cell. All I saw during my days is these four plain white walls. At night when I played in bed, I use to just stare at the ceiling. Although these walls and ceilings were nothing but plain and blank. My mind added so much colour to it. I started thinking about all the ideas and possibilities that the world could have. It was like my mind was projecting a hologram of all the amazing inventions I was designing in my head. At that moment I didn't know where life would take me in fact till this day I still don't know. Even right now I am sitting in a café writing this. And all the people around me have no idea. Sometimes it gets boring writing at home, you need to get out more and see different places, be in different atmosphere. I take my creativity wherever I go.

You know when I really think about it, I could have

been anything I wanted. I could have been a comedian, actor, entertainer, gamer etc. But why did I choose to be someone that will help people and bring goodness to the people of this world? Well I know there is enough of entertainers and comedians in the world and we no longer need that. We need thinkers and helpers. I don't know but there is something about me that has no attachment to being selfish. I'm so selfless I'm always ready to sacrifice my pleasure to make someone's day. Maybe it's because of everything I've been through that has made me this way.

I view this world as something that might not be here tomorrow. I'm constantly asking myself, what is it that truly drives me? When I watch a video of an orphan child sending a message to their dead parents saying, "I love you mum and dad, I wish you was here, to play with me or eat with me, I miss you." That hits me so hard. And in my head I'm saying don't worry I'm coming. I mean what is that child going through? The broken buildings in the background and no food or someone to look after them. While I sleep In a warm bed, that child will be sleeping outside somewhere tonight, or they might not even sleep because of the fear an attack because their country is at civil war etc. what if the charity money we are giving (that if you are giving charity) how do you know its actually going to that cause? Instead of donating money blindly not know where it's going, why don't we go to these places and actually help people physically. I mean I see no excuses. You are able to go on a resort island for a holiday every year, so why can't you take out 1 week or even 4 days to go to a small village and help them improve their living conditions? Well if you are thinking I don't have time for that, you need to go through law etc. making all these excuses. Just know that tomorrow you could wake up and be I'm the same position as them. And then you will praying that someone out there has some time to come and help you out. What you have been given in this life is a blessing but also a test. It is a test to see how you would use that blessing. Don't take it for granted. Look at it this way, a millionaire and someone that is struggling for some air (someone that Is not a millionaire), at the end of the day they both will have the same grave and be under the same soil. Who are you trying to impress? Who are you showing off for? What will you gain by doing what you are doing? Have you forgotten about those who need you? Have you forgotten that there are others out there in the world that are struggling? So what will you do?

It hurts me so much to watch videos like this to see that there is so little people on the world that are actually helping the poor and needy. Even in London there is a lot people struggling we are not helping them.

I watched so many videos like this, even videos of homeless people on the streets of America or United Kingdom. At first before I realised that I was a helper, fighter, world changer or even just a good human being. I thought that being this wasn't cool. Like who would like someone that talks about sadness and all this other deep talks. Who would look up to me if I was giving food to the homeless.

Rather than wearing a £1000 shirt and driving a nice car? But as time went on I witnessed that the world was just getting worse and worse. The world is messed up and it has made the people messed up. However I know there are still good people out there, that are trying their best to make this place a better place to live. As time went on I realised that being a good human being was rare, no one was doing that any more. No one was helping each other out any more. As time went by the world became more and more selfish, greedy and in Pursue of wealth. Everyone wanted money or some sort of gain. If they don't get anything from it they won't do it.

People that take their time out to spread positivity and wisdom about helpfulness and goodness. People that build that type of foundation that can make someone cry happy tears because you saved them. That's the type of people we need. Beautiful & powerful souls that bring goodness to the hearts of people. Showing acts of kindness and showing actions that others can do too.

For once let's stop thinking about what we can gain from it and start thinking about how others can gain from your actions. I mean if we don't help each other? then who will? If you do something for someone expecting them to give you something in return, does not that make you feel guilty? Let's face it, no matter how cold and heartless you want to act. We all know deep down you do care. So stop putting on an act that is not you.

Versions of life

So many things I have to deal with,
Trapped in a loop
Sometimes I forgot to eat,
because life makes me work so hard

For something that should be mine,

Sometimes life shows you no other way,
Sometimes life makes you forget
The purpose to why you are here,
Sometimes life shows you death as a better way,
But then god reminds you that it's all a test,
So don't worry and just make sure you live it right,

Give me a mic & I'll tell you about the life people live,
Give me a camera & I'll show the reality of success,
Give me a pen & I'll write books for you to read,
Show me your troubles
And I'll tell you there is nothing better then kindness,

Everyone is looking for something
But don't know where to find it,
Maybe it's a long search
That should take time till you
Define it,

We all have our own definitions
You just have to make sure
You are in the right mind frame,

Because without knowledge and respect
There is no guidance,

So tell me what is your version of life
And how will you find peace,
Because a mind that is scribbled
Is a mind in confinement.

Relationships and moving on

I always watched people around me tear each other apart. Mostly those who are family. A lot of broken relationships. Brothers and sisters falling apart, parents and children no longer speaking to each other, uncles, cousins, you name it. Even those who are not family. I also became one of those who breaks relationships. But with me it is different. I only break and move away from those poisonous relationships. Whether you are my uncle, aunty, cousin or even my friend, if you bring negativity and I see that all you are doing is holding me back, then I'll have no choice but to cut you off. I've become really good at that now and I am very picky with who I let be in my presence. I am that type of person when I have seen and heard enough, I'm gone. At times I'm just thinking about cutting everyone off, yes that will mean I will be alone but I know I'll be happy. I don't have to worry about caring for anyone, worry about being understood or liked and most importantly I don't have always explain myself. At a very young age I realised that, why am I trying so hard to hold on to people? Why am I trying to make things work? And why am I trying to please everyone? Most of the time people underestimate me and misunderstand me. The other times is that they think they will benefit more by betraying me than being loyal to me. I mean even I know that some things are not meant to be. There is always things that will go wrong especially people.

So many people just let me down to be honest, like I expected so much more from them. I had so much respect for those people but they are unable to see that it took us so long to build this bond. They are unable to notice that special connection we had, you know why our energy was so good. They are so focused on that little problem or issue we had that they are ready to throw away everything. It all comes down to the pain we feel. When someone hurts you really bad. Even you don't feel like holding on to that bond. Because of the pain, the disappointment and the hurt. I went from the world resolves around people, to the world resolves around me. My world is what I make it to be.

It Is so easy to ruin a relationship today, people just don't care any more. Well I gave up with holding onto something that is no good for me. I see it as a sacrifice I have to make in order to be happy and move on. I spent most of my days alone, enjoying my own company and my own peace of mind. I have become so used to it that if you told me, that tomorrow I had to leave everything and go.

I would go, even though it will hurt, I will still go and live on an island. However we as humans we need each other, otherwise we forget all the ways that makes us humans. We need love, we need communication, we need friends that we can trust and we need those who make life seem like something to fight for.

Unfortunately there are some people who get jealous of you, some people who want to see you do well but not better then them, some people who say they got your back when they don't, some people who smile in your face but talk bad about you when you are not there and those who don't care about you at all but themselves.

These are the type of people who will just use you, take advantage of you or just waste your time and do what they please with the bond you currently have. It does feel good to just let go and move on. Like you don't even need them in your life. Now if someone says anything to me or breaks the bond we have, I just simply tell them to never call me, don't text me, don't follow what I do, don't worry about what I am doing or how I am and simply get the hell out of my face and don't come back!

With my family a lot of things is broken, I no longer speak with anyone from my dads Side any more. Even with few people from my mothers side too. Believe me it is way better now that they are not part of my life. Even two or three of my close friends that I grew up, literally that I thought were my family even though they are not. I no longer speak with them and now want nothing with that. I've just moved on, yes it hurt and also felt good, I know this is right for me. It has given me more motivation and made me feel way more happy as I feel more focused on myself. I felt like I had a lot on my chest and finally I'm feel lighter and more of myself. They have hurt me a lot and therefore I want nothing to do with them. I'm in rage but at the same time calm.

The way I look at it is this bad poison slime kind of thing that was infecting me and holding me back. It drowned me in darkness and strangled me till I fidgeted for breath. And there I stand looking at the old me that didn't let go. I look at the new me I feel clean, I feel more in control of my life like there is no one here telling me where to go, I feel more happy, I feel more loved, I feel more connected with my creator and most importantly I feel more free. I know it is not the end of the world if someone does not like you or if you don't get along with someone. It is not the end of the world if you have ended a relationship. You need to stop caring about things that don't really matter and learn to live for yourself.

It is priorities, you are prioritising that you are the most important person and your happiness comes first. Let me ask you something, if tomorrow your wife, girlfriend, husband or lover woke up and suddenly said I don't want to be with you any more? What would you do? Would you try to make it work and make them stay with you? Or would you just say that's fine I respect your decision, please grab your things and leave thanks, I have nothing else to say to you. This might sound cold but if you are at this certain level which I can't explain to you, but it will be that easy for you to say. Why force someone to stay with you when they don't want to? If they really loved you, wouldn't they stay anyway? Matter of fact would that thought even come to their head in the first place?

Today, there are people out there who are together, but not In love, and there are people who are in love, but are not together.

I got a lot of enemies and I got a lot of people pretending like they loyal to me. The thing is? They actually think they have the upper hand here. I'll let time decide that.

There was a lot of people that I thought they really had my back, that they truly respected the relationship we had. What hurts and makes me angry is that the person you had years of connection with, is unable to understand you. And the person you met couple of months ago understands you better. It shows that all this time they didn't really pay attention to you like you thought they did, otherwise they would know you and understand you properly.

I am really good at building healthy relationships but I am also really good at ending them and then making sure you regret it. Aha. I thought all the people I knew we was cool but you wanted to take advantage of my kindness. well, now deal with what you asked for. Yes I am indirecting this to all those people. So if you are one of those who want to hate on me and your reading this now just know I did exactly what I said.

I can be very salty, stubborn and arrogant when I need to be. That's only if you get on my bad side. It's good, it's good for business and good for survival.

I ended my relationship with the woman I called aunty, and anyone that is associated with her. Even her daughters I thought they actually loved me and treated me as their little brother. But now when I put some things together and put the missing puzzle pieces together it makes sense. That it was all fake love. They brought all these nice toys for me and games but were they being sincere? Did they really buy it for me because they truly loved me and cared for me? Or was it so that in the future they can say they did this and that for me.

When I think about these things it makes me so mad and in rage, like I just can't trust anyone like them. Even when their dad passed away, I went to see him and pay my respects. That man was the only one I liked in their whole family. I went to the hospital and to the house afterwards, not one of them even spoke to me. It is a day for Grief and you are meant to forget and forgive anyone. Even if your worst enemy turned up, just for that day, you are meant to forget that and respect them for coming and showing everyone respect regardless of the situation. It was at this moment I realised who they truly were.

It's like that saying I always say, you want to know someone true colours go against them and see how they react. You can learn a lot of the way they react and what type of person they are.

After all I'm crazy at reading people so this was like my second nature. The only person who came unto and spoke was one of the daughters husband. He put his arm around me, while walking, and said something like hope you are happy, I think he even swore at me and then said don't ever come back. I can't remember it clearly because straight after that moment I was so mad and angry, I was fuming and my body was heated I don't know what I would have done if didn't control myself. I respected that guy so much all these years and I finally saw who he really was, all those nice things he used to say to me and those advises. What a hypocrite!

Maybe he forgot but I was a crazy guy back then, quiet but a psycho. I mean he is not the only person who knew people, I can get dirty work done without actually getting my hands dirty, maybe he forgot that I was out on the roads selling stuff and living "gangster" or maybe he does not even know. I changed and left that life behind me, but that does not mean that side to me is gone. It is still here, I still do those things just more professionally and legally. If you want a problem with me, I have no problem bringing you the solution. Aha!.

I have a really small circle, I am careful who I let around me. I don't trust anyone, I only trust on professional basis when It comes to running my business, but with my personal life? I don't trust anyone.

Till this day that scene still sticks in my head and makes me boil every time. I love it! Gives me urgency, motivation and power. The more people try to walk over me? The more I give them new shoes to do it with, then afterwards tax them for it.

The reason why I am saying all of this, is that sometimes breaking a relationship is good. Because it makes you wiser, stronger and makes you realise that you are the most important person in the room. If you feel like you don't belong there? Get yourself out of there and don't look back.

Like my good friend Hannah says, "you have as much rights as anyone else to be in the room."

You have to know who deserves to be in your presence and who does not. Watch how all those people regret and wish that they was on my good side when I am successful, rich and whatever that may burn them inside. ha!

Now I am so happy, I am living life happily, on my terms

and finally free. I don't have to worry about having negative, venomous and downgrading people in my life any more.

'I know what I want and I'm coming to get mine.'

Cursed

Maybe my dad cursed me,
Yes so many people hurt me,

So many people want to see me fail,
And guess what I'm failing,
Even my family didn't care where I went,
It's always dark here and it's raining,

What's blood when water is better,
And what's water when blood is like a mirror, trying to survive in this weather,
All this is a hidden message to my save me letter,

They doubted me so I tried but I can't,
When everyone is out to get you,
But a happy family is all I want,
I never gave up and I never ran,

I'm stuck in this beautiful curse,
Where nothing goes right & your always hurt,
They want me to loose and they want me to burn,
So now I'm wondering will my life ever make a turn,

Everything seems like it's in rewind,
It's not getting easy,
But the only powerful thing I have is my mind, take
me to that happy place take me where it is nice,

Life is what you make it, but that seems like a lie,
Everything I was told I applied,
But maybe everything I was told is a lie?

How do I break out of this illusion,
How do I stop hearing these cries,
How do I break out of this curse,
Because clearly this is not a fairytale filled with
smiles,

I'm just tired of living this life,
Where we have to work like slaves,
And eventually die, and we retire with regrets, living
the last of our days just trying to survive,

There are so many people that are jealous & hate on
me,
Like why! don't you breathe the same air as me?

And it's like they give you these opportunities just to see you lose,
Or maybe I am just cursed because people are cruel,

Why don't we stop all the war and fighting, and actually help each other succeed, because violence is the answer to suffer in defeat,

are you real or fake just showing everyone different faces,
I'm cursed and my mind is always in different places.

Here is the thing, people will say what they want, people will do what they want, people will get jealous, people will try to do anything to ruin and damage your self image. For years I had to hear people talk bad about me, about my family and about my mum. There is a lot of people out there that will show you they are interested in what you are telling them but under that fake picture, they are actually burning inside, with jealousy, envy and just want to see you loose. They will wish bad and pray bad for you. I am not saying everyone out there is like that but unfortunately majority of the people out there are. The good news is that we can change this. The bad news is a lot of people do not want to.

'Speak it into the universe & it will come into existence'.

My ultimate future goal.

The cold dancing air hits my face, it is comforting like as if it is almost calming all the nerves in my head. A fresh aroma from the atmosphere welcomes my humble presence. I can hear a soothing Erhu playing a melody for the strings, that attach my soul to this world. Making sure every note to my heart is played correctly. Everything seems to be in order and in balance as I sit on this cushion made, long, folded grass. Colour of bright green grass hug my pupils, as if it had longed to see it for many years. Fragile as it can be the leafs slowly wonder away as they take its leave from the tree. Floating to where ever their next destination may be.

I can see an inviting blue clear ocean in the distance, where the reflection of the almost gone sunrise leaves its mark.

An open field of greenery with different portions solely existing for different purposes. One portion is the vegetables that bring me my relief of survival, the other portions are, a flower garden to let me know all the different representations of life, the animals, the birds and the harmony of the sky, let me know all the different edges to life. A smell of wood, like it is just been cut, slowly taking the form of a beautiful house. A Japanese style sliding door with a open front porch complimenting its wide size. Front garden to surround its uniqueness of the one floor house. A pond covered with parts of lily pads and foot size stones for its borders. Small pathway leading out of the surrounding fence that is protecting the closeness beauty of the porch. Near the corner just inside the fence, stands a teenage cherry blossom tree, still growing to its full potential. Reminds me of how crooked you can be and look when you are going through the process of growth. But once you have grown only mesmerisation lives. Silent but whispering of nature does not make me feel lonely. The absorbing views and the soft warm soil underneath the sole of my feet, make me forget where I came from, why I was so unhappy, what was troubling me and what was tearing me away.

There is no memories before this place. My heart is at last at peace for this was the dream it yarned for it to be true. I feel empty and free, weighing the same as paper and blank as it can be.

Everything here is enjoying its own company just like me, but every now and then we tell each other stories, we laugh and just breathe. I sometimes lay down on this huge open field, observing the sky. Taking a nap knowing I am safe. As I wake up to the heat of the sun, all types of little insects celebrate around me, happy to see me. Everything seems so clear and meaningful.

Why was I so worried about the other place when this

was all I needed. I feel as everything has been washed away, I feel new and feel at home. The changing directions of the wind gives me bursts of energy. The quiet world around me makes me understand why I am happy. The mountains on the other side far away from me and the forest likewise, give me hope of exploration and adventure. There is so much to discover with my creative mind. There is so much to find every time you follow these flies. The scent is so attractive you can fall in love every time. Not bothered by any imperfections, the plants show that equality can be found without any hesitation. A seed can only grow the way it has been raised and the trees can only give fruits if it is destined.

When I finally become rich and wealthy I can finally move onto my next big goal. I would like to buy an island one day, build a city and give these orphans, unfortunate people, homeless people a place to live. I would also like to create my own healthcare system, education system, a place where engineering, architecture, inventions and creativity can take place without any limits. This place will be like a different planet, a futuristic island that will advance the world by decades.

I want to create a environment that money is not the

priority, where money does not make the world go around. Believe it or not, but our planet is dying. It is only a matter of time before we perish with our own foolishness. I just think a lot of people have forgotten the true reason to living. Everyone is so worried about making a living on the surface, they forget that the surface also needs a reason to exist. That cannot happen if we are all ruining the very thing we call our homes. I want to be able to help all the people that have gone struggle, I made a promise that I will do good with all the money I have. I mean someone has to right? I feel like everything that has happened to me so far, have prepared me for a very important future. I have a big role, just reserved for me. All the greats have gone and passed away. All the greats that have changed the world on an unimaginable levels. Now the world is waiting for the next great to come along and take us to the next phase. Who knows it might even be me in the next 20 years. Even if it is not me, I hope people support that great.

I would like to create so many games, create my own anime, create my own TV series, have my own talk show, invent futuristic technologies, have my own foundation that tackles world hunger, introduce new ways of teaching, work on city architecture, a complete new sustainable design, have a big family of people that I have helped over the world, do talks in front of millions of people, show people that you can make lasting beauty happen regardless where you come from and what colour your skin is.

I want to do everything I have said and even more, so next time when a poor, broken, damaged and helpless boy like me says I want to make something of myself? I will make sure they do. Because although they might have nothing all I see is a unstoppable soul still smiling with a pocket full of dreams and treasures.

I am that poor boy that still dreams until I no longer matter, an incomplete story till I am no longer here.

Mum if it is written for me and if my creator wills, then I will do everything I can to make you proud.

'Make sure your story has a meaning, even the world wouldn't want to forget.'